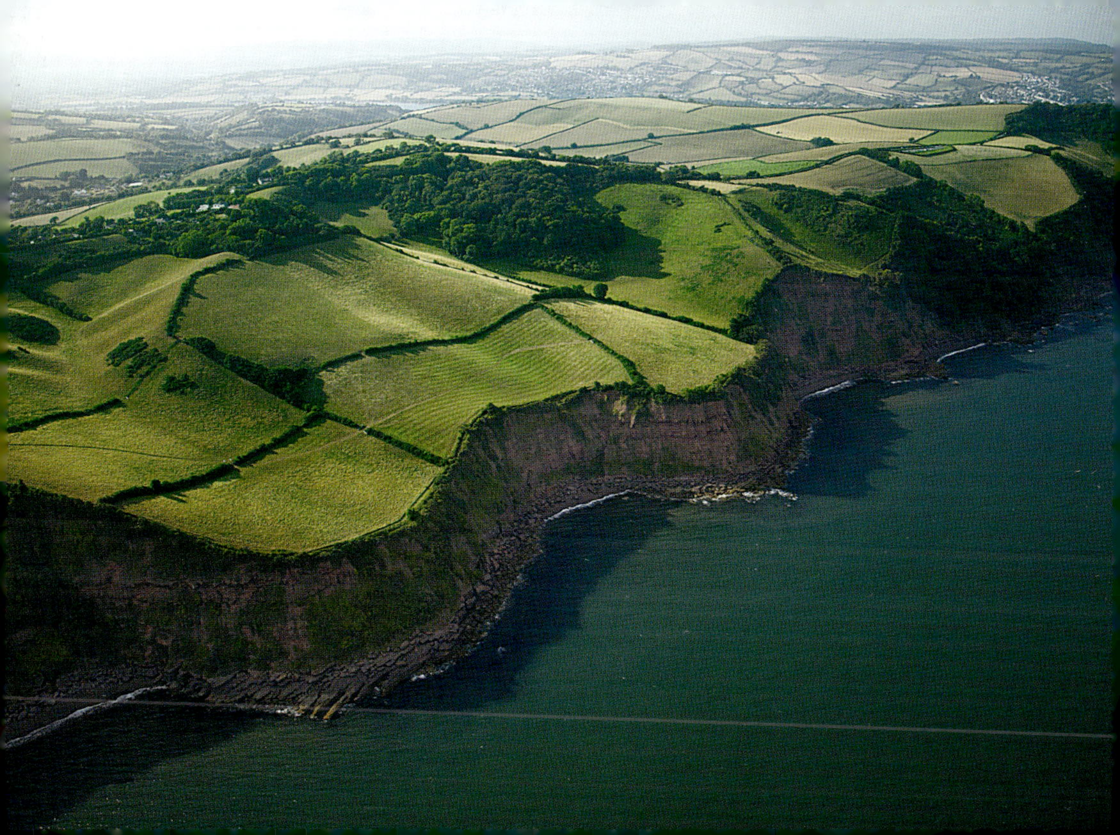

SOUTH DEVON & THE ENGLISH RIVIERA

Photographs by Bob Croxford

South Devon enjoys a mild climate which has attracted residents and visitors for many years. With its piers and beaches, harbours and wooded valleys the area has much to offer.

Published by Atmosphere
Willis Vean
Mullion Cornwall TR12 7DF
England
Tel 01326 240180
email info@atmosphere.co.uk

ISBN 0 9543409 3 0

Printed and bound in Italy

Frontispiece Aerial view of the South Devon coast near Shaldon

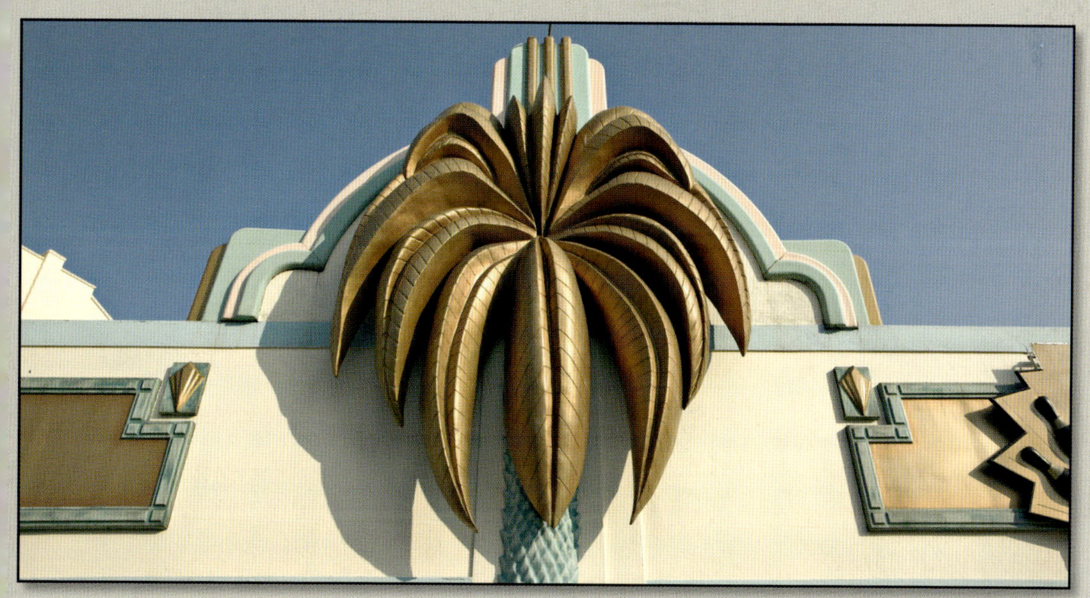

Amusement Arcade in TORQUAY

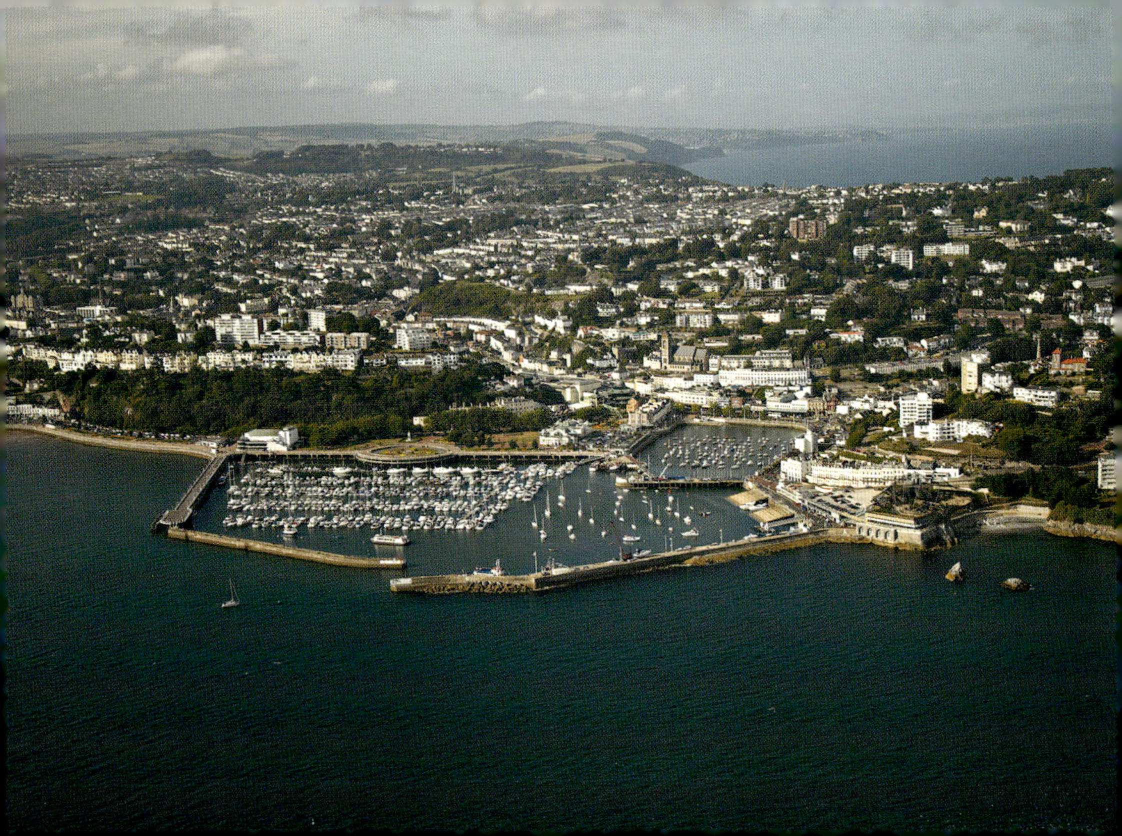

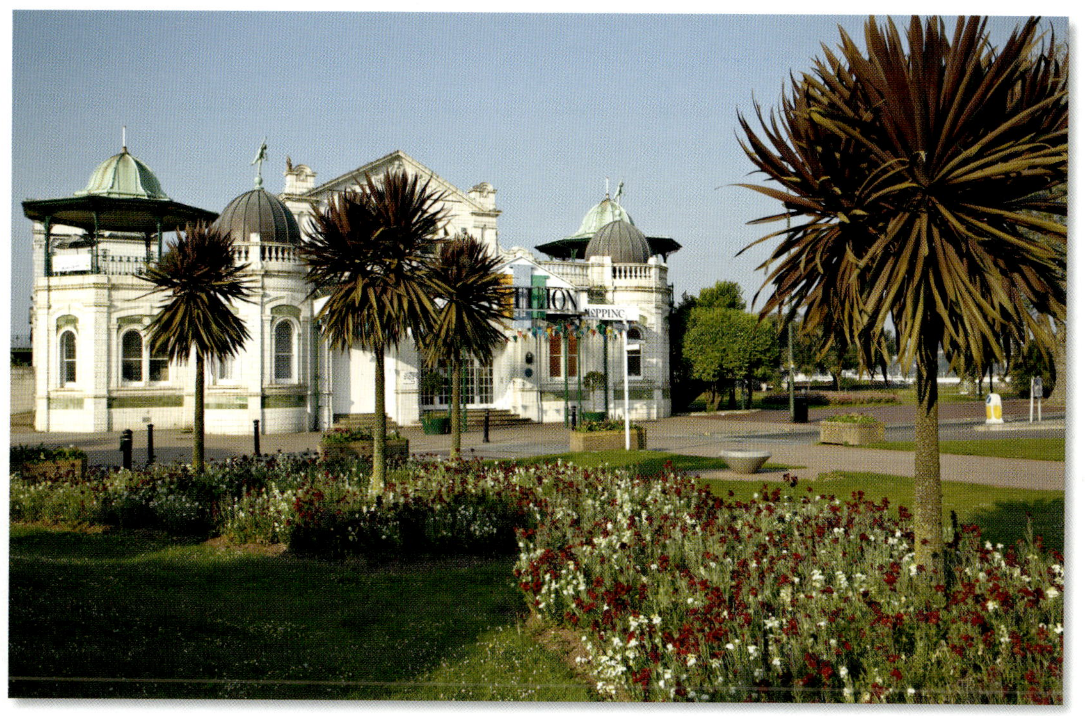

Aerial view of TORQUAY. In the distance the sweep of coastline to the Exe Estuary

The Pavilion in TORQUAY

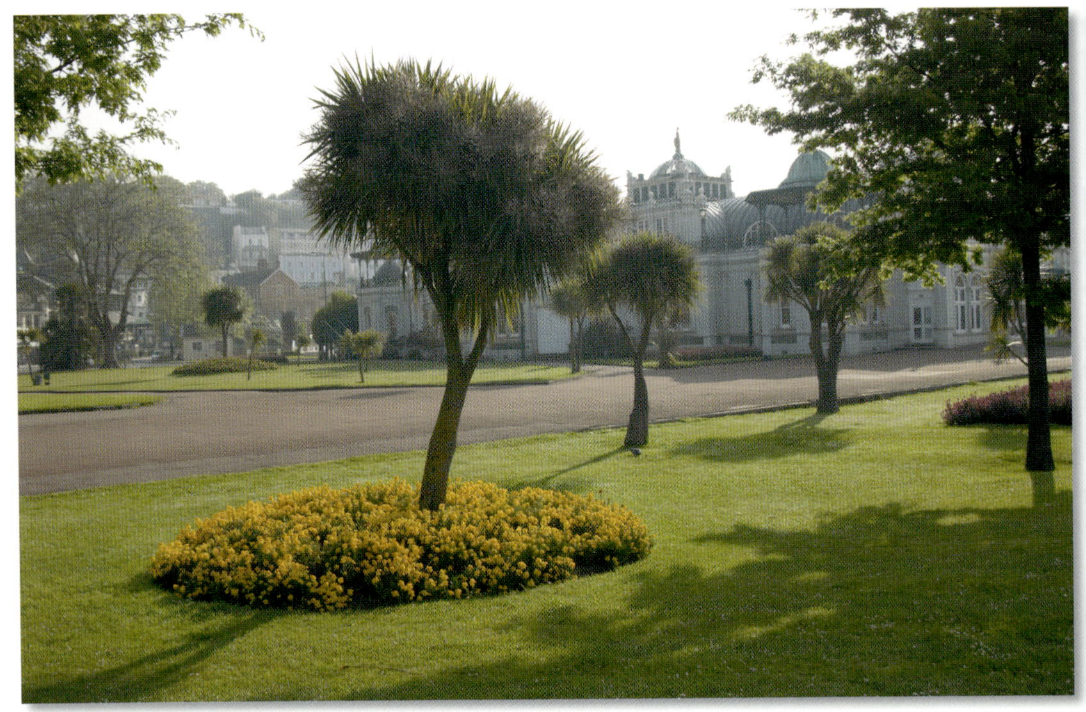

Early morning in the Princess Gardens, TORQUAY

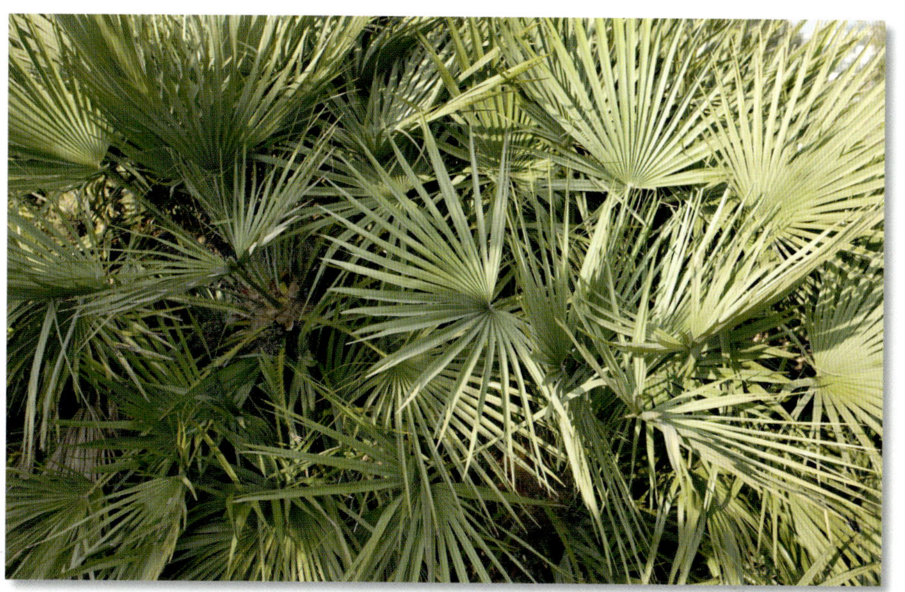

Tropical plants thrive in SOUTH DEVON'S mild climate

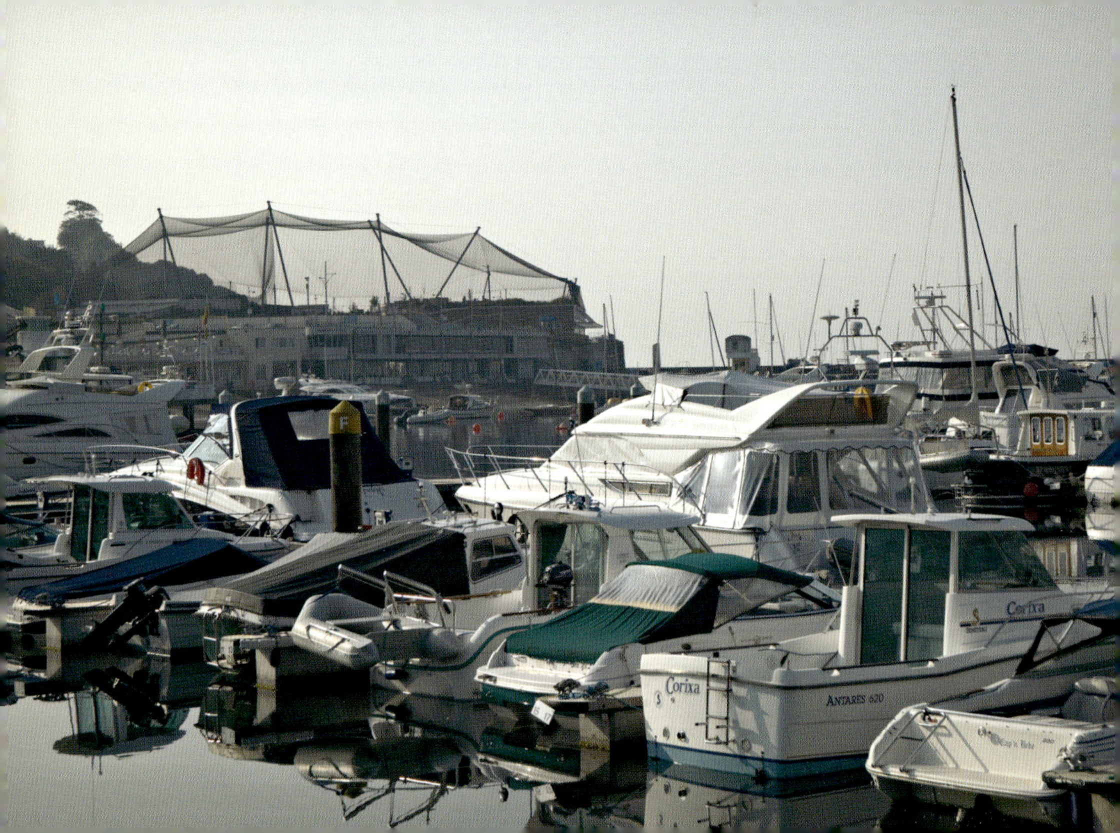
F
Corixa
Corixa
ANTARES 620

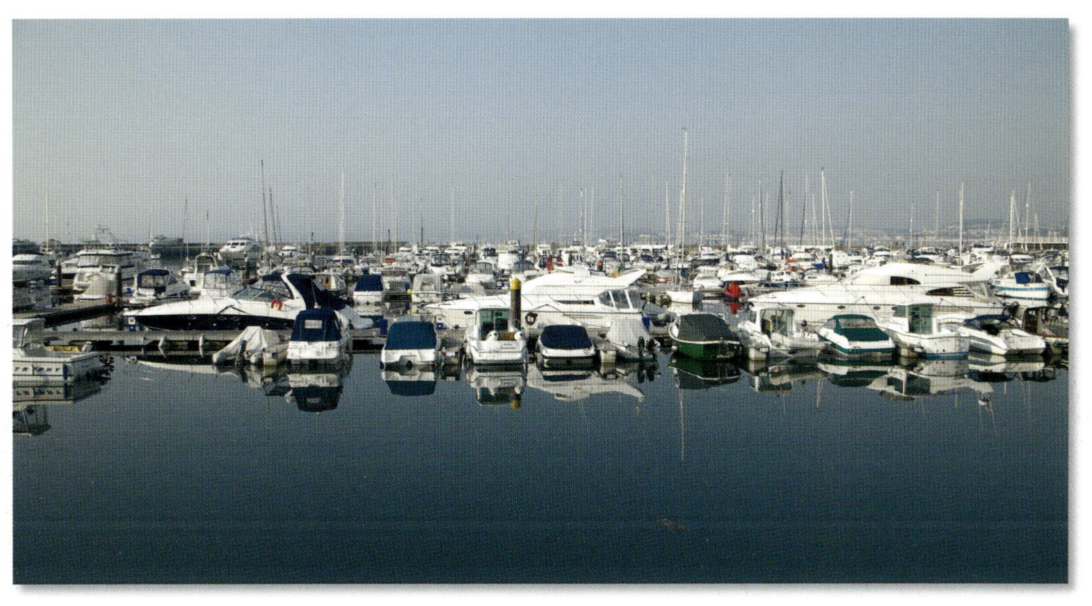

The Marina in TORQUAY with 'Living Waters' in the background

Blue and white nautical colours

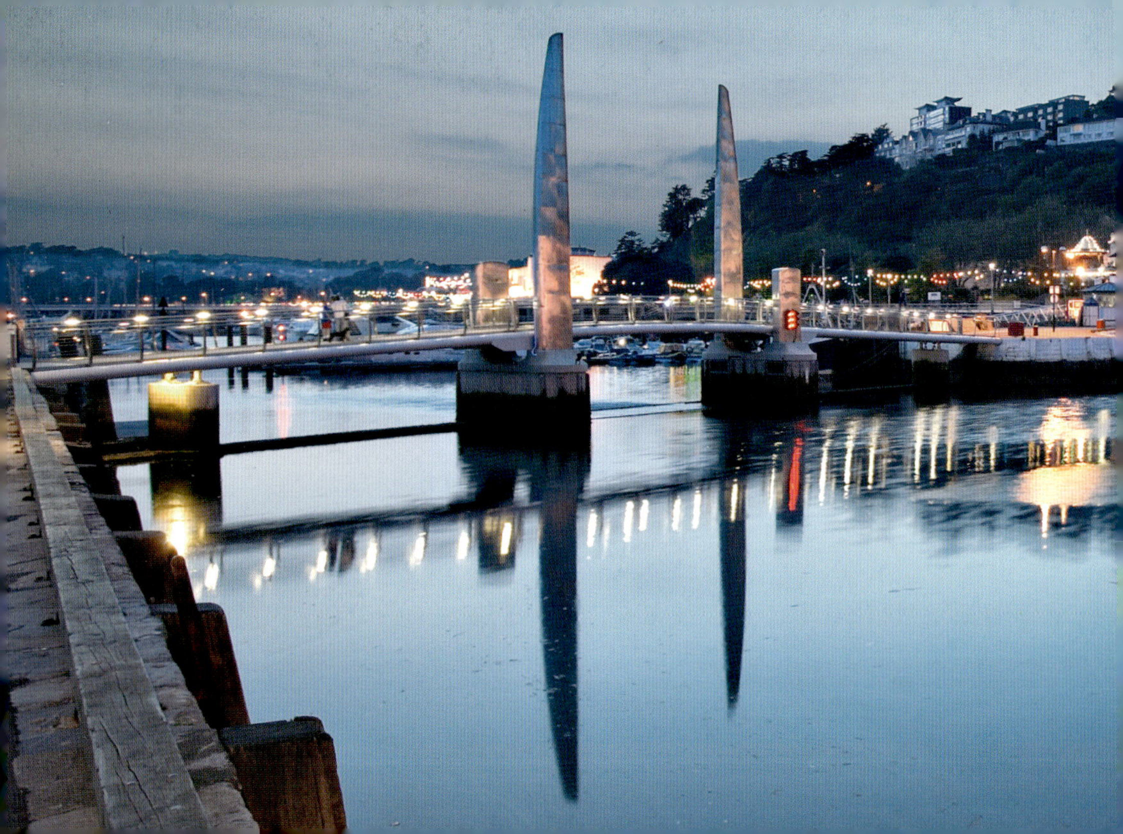

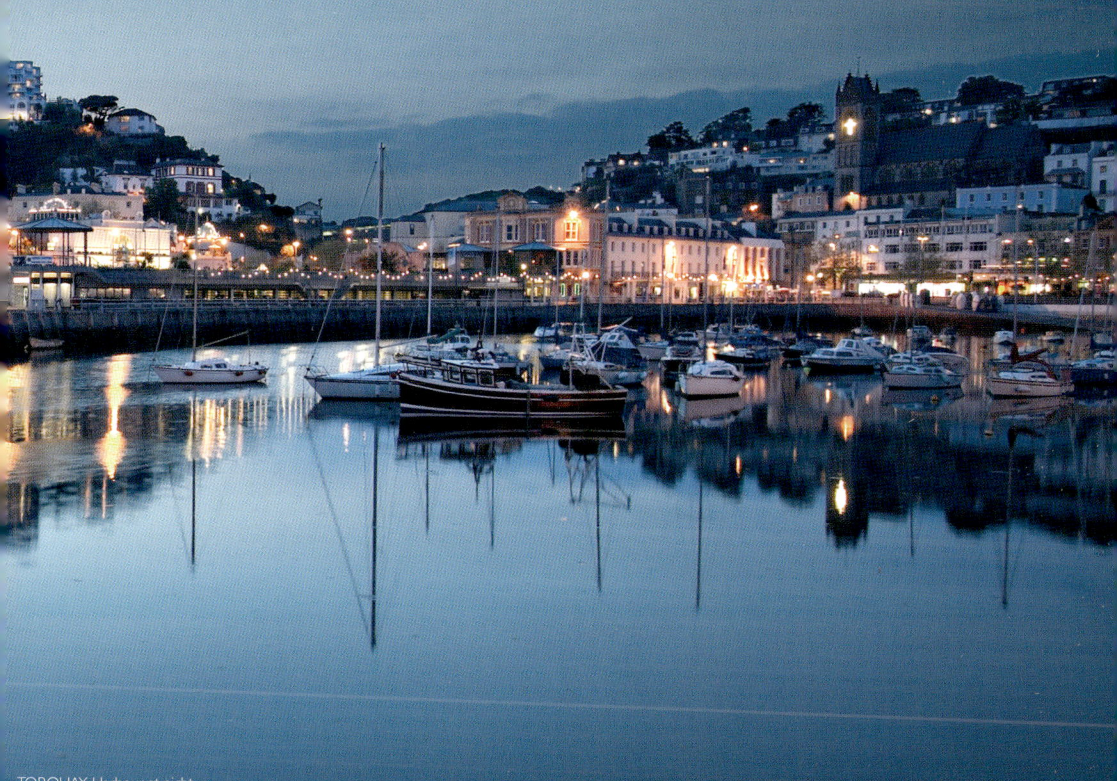

TORQUAY Harbour at night

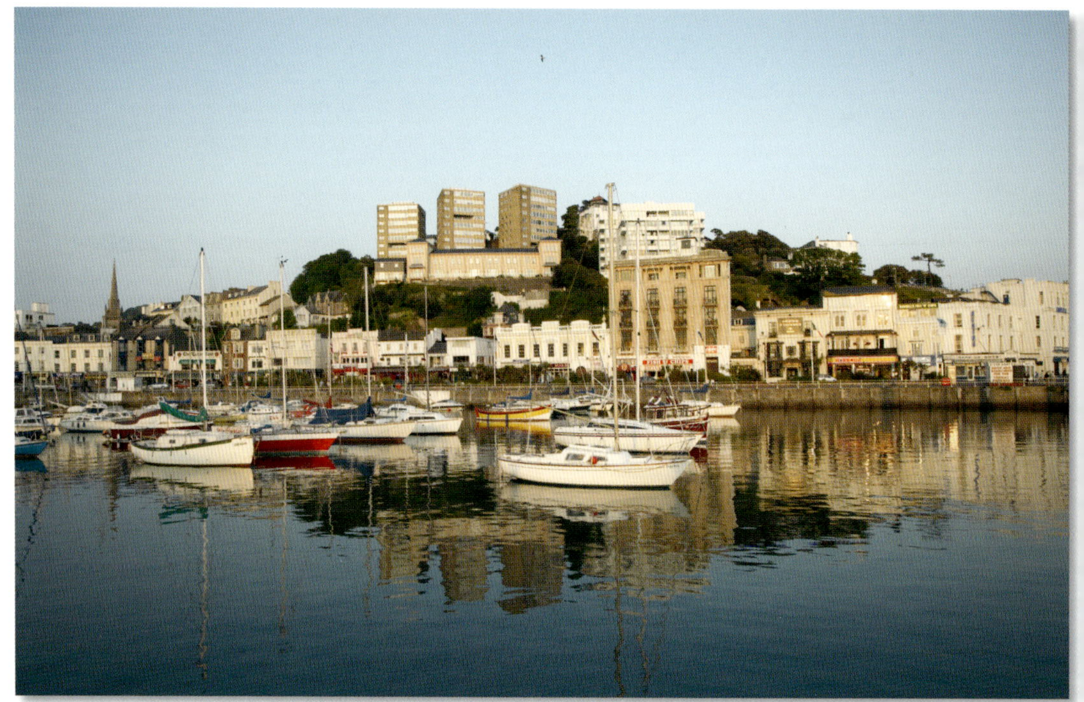

The inner harbour reflects boats and VICTORIA PARADE

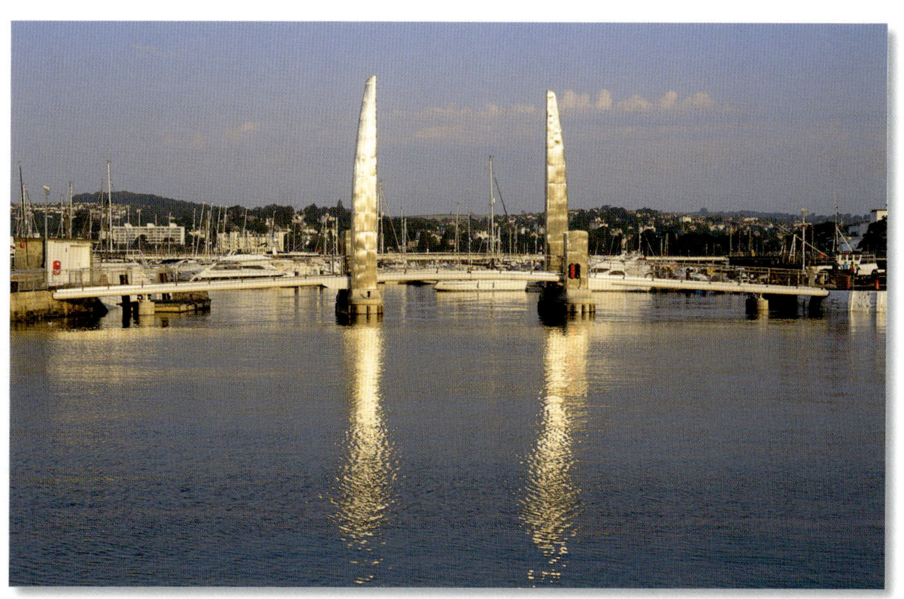

The New Harbour Bridge enclosing TORQUAY'S inner harbour

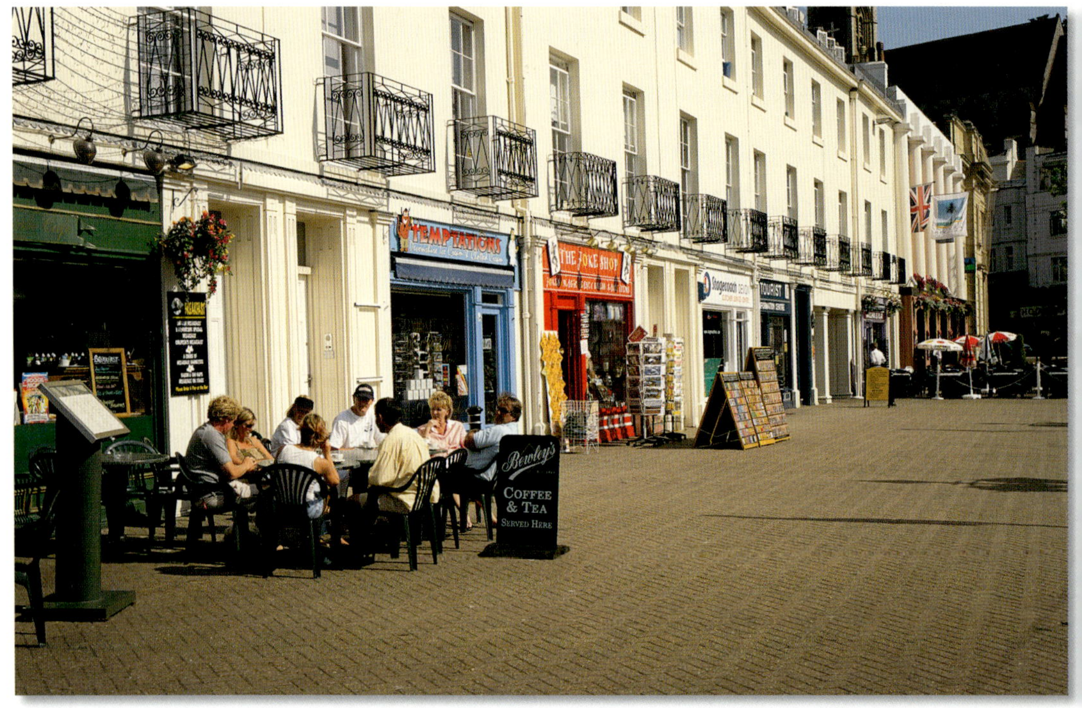

Continental style on VAUGHAN PARADE

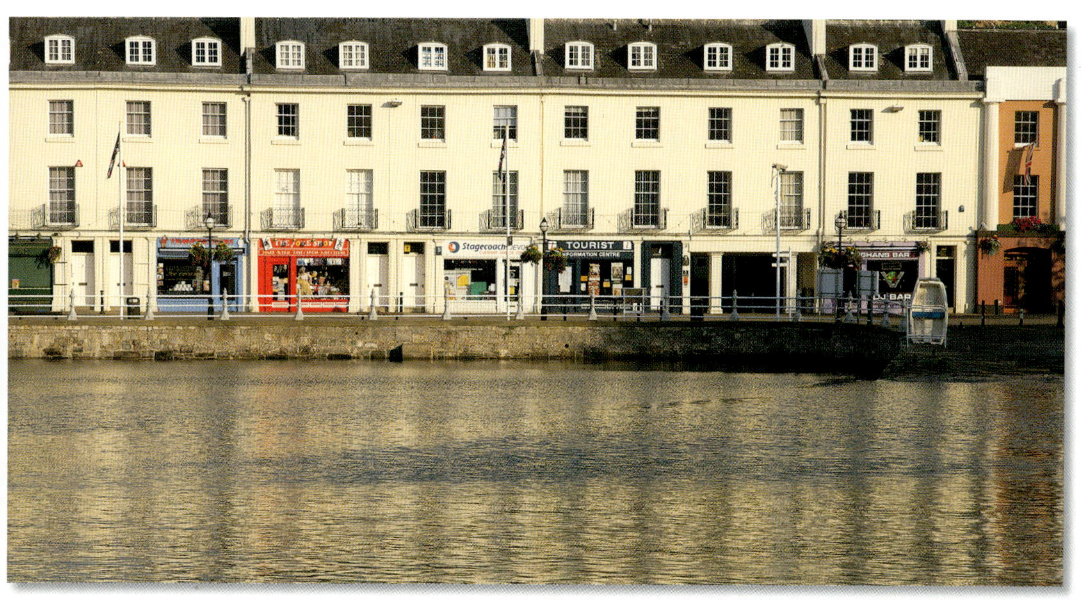

VAUGHAN PARADE reflected in the harbour

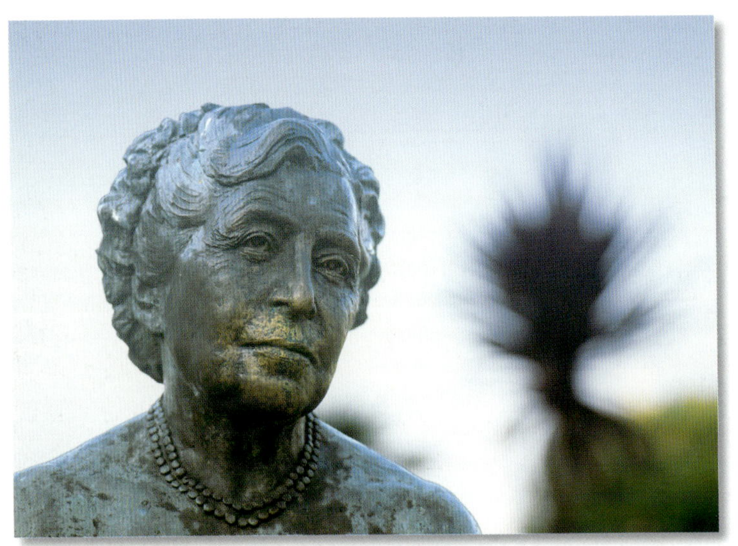

Bronze of Torquay's famous resident, AGATHA CHRISTIE

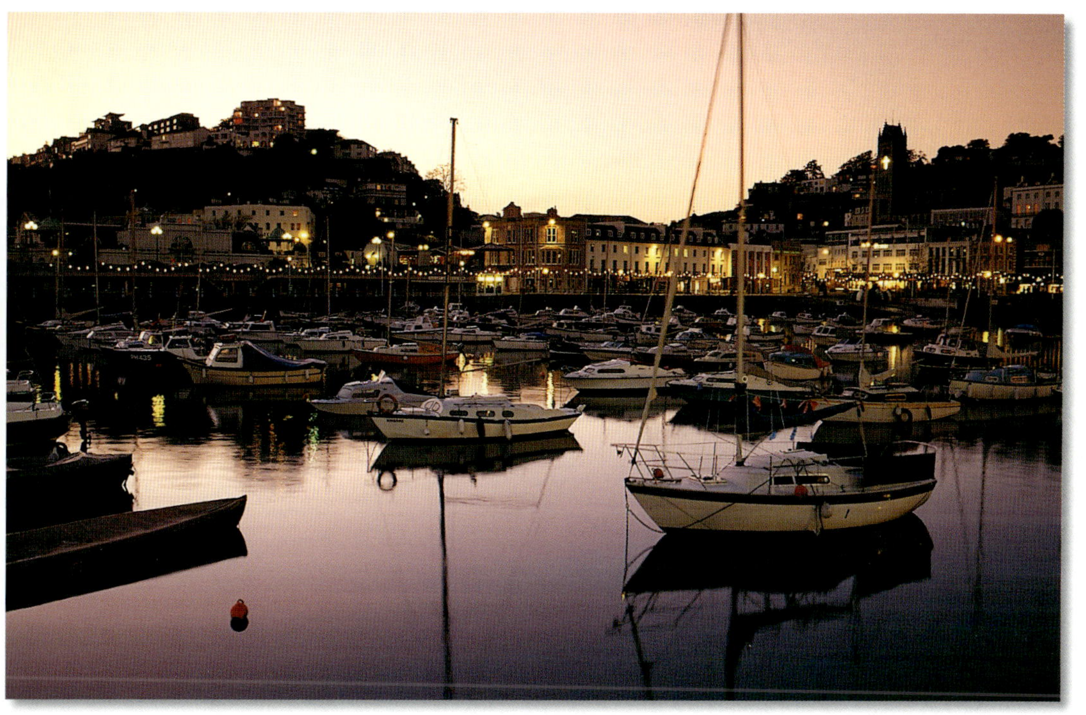

The inner harbour at twilight

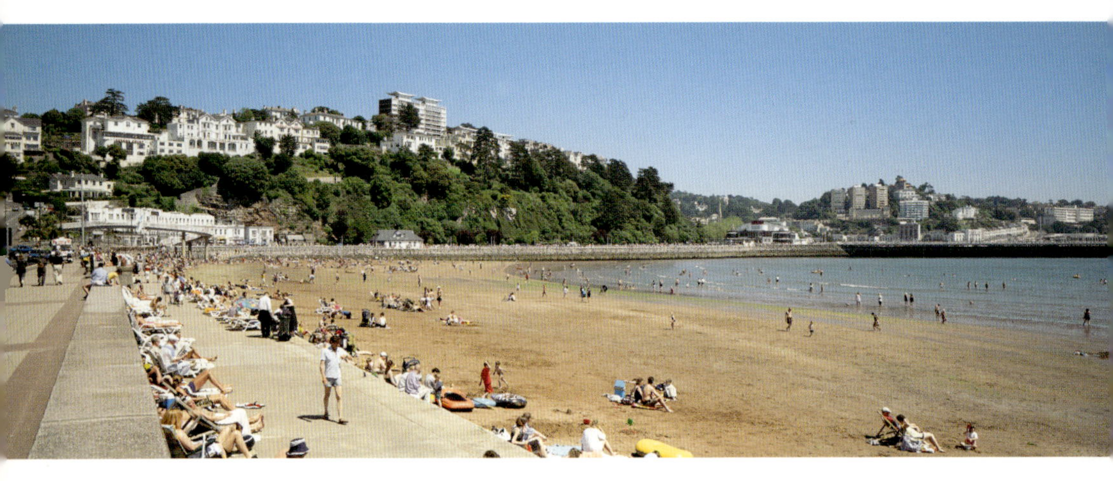

TORRE ABBEY SANDS is a popular beach in the heart of Torquay

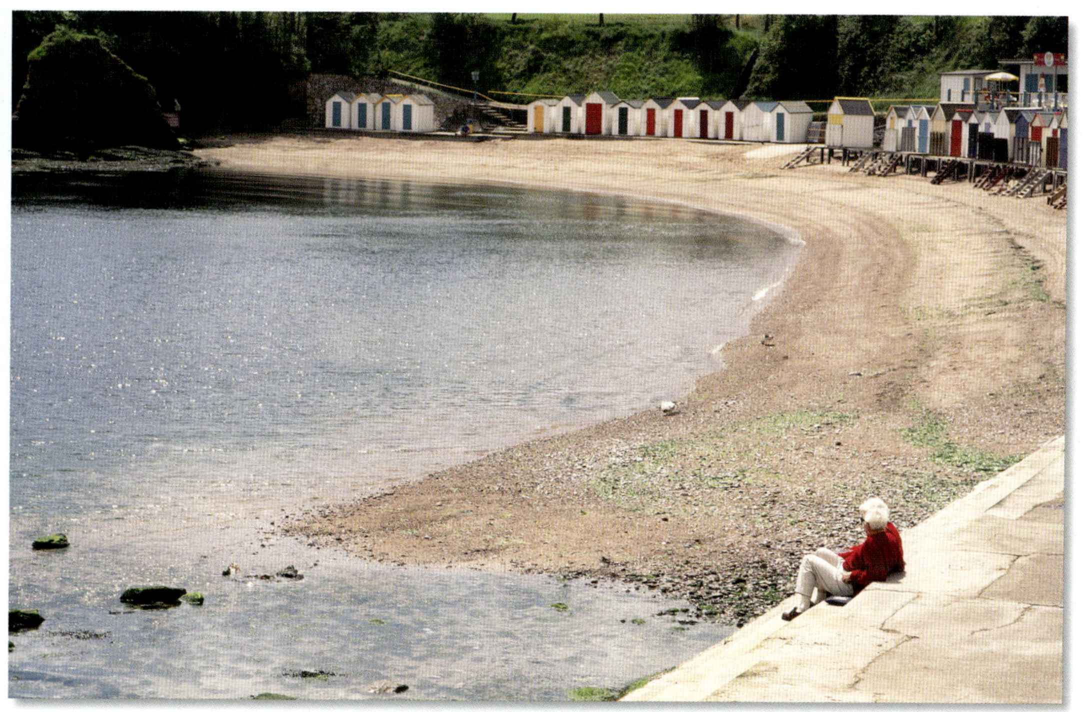

A quiet spot in the sun

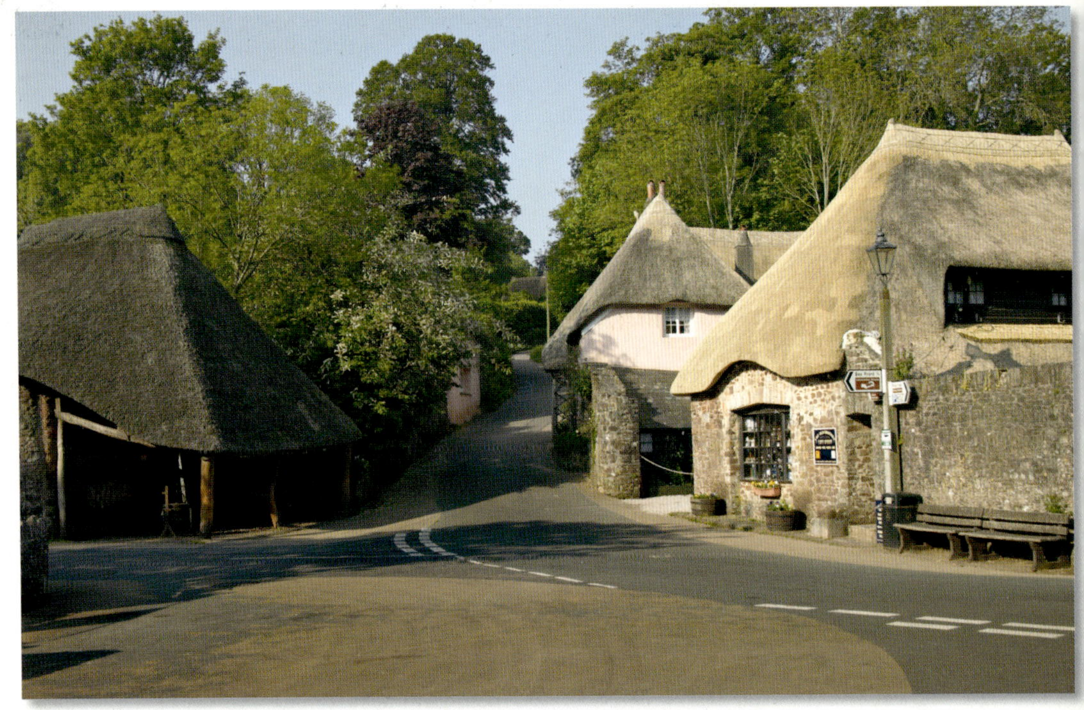

THE OLD FORGE at Cockington

ROSE COTTAGE

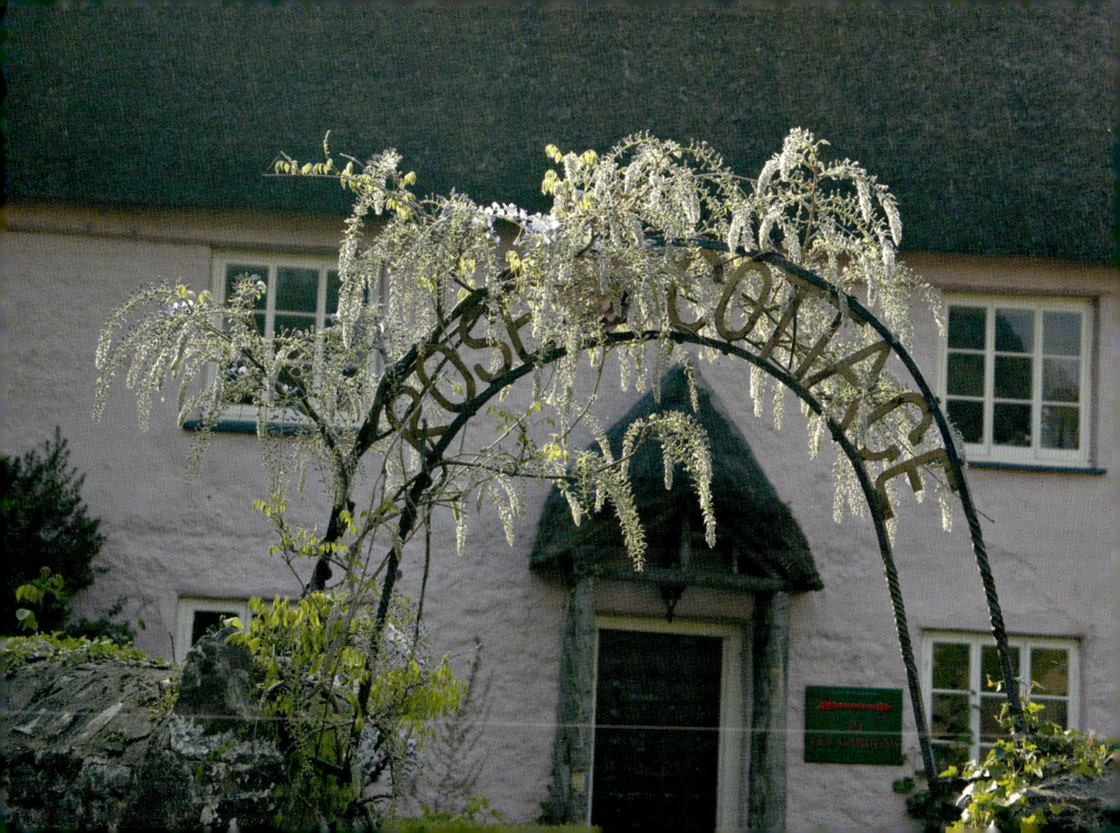
ROSE COTTAGE

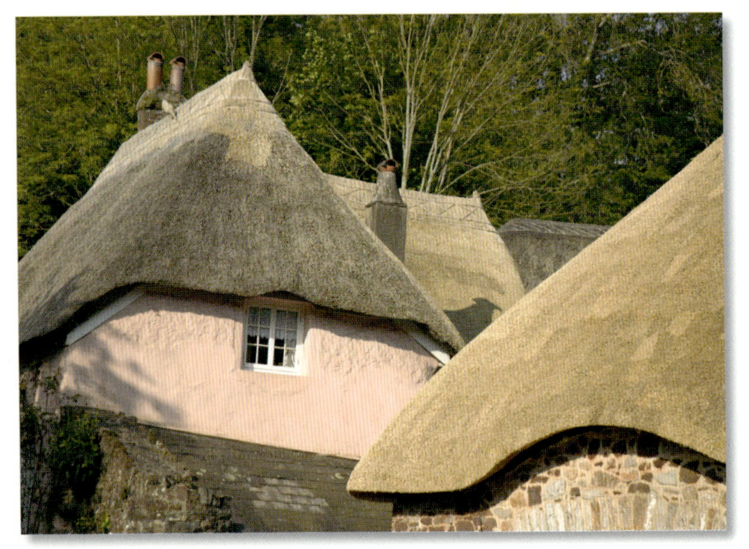

Thatched roofs at Cockington

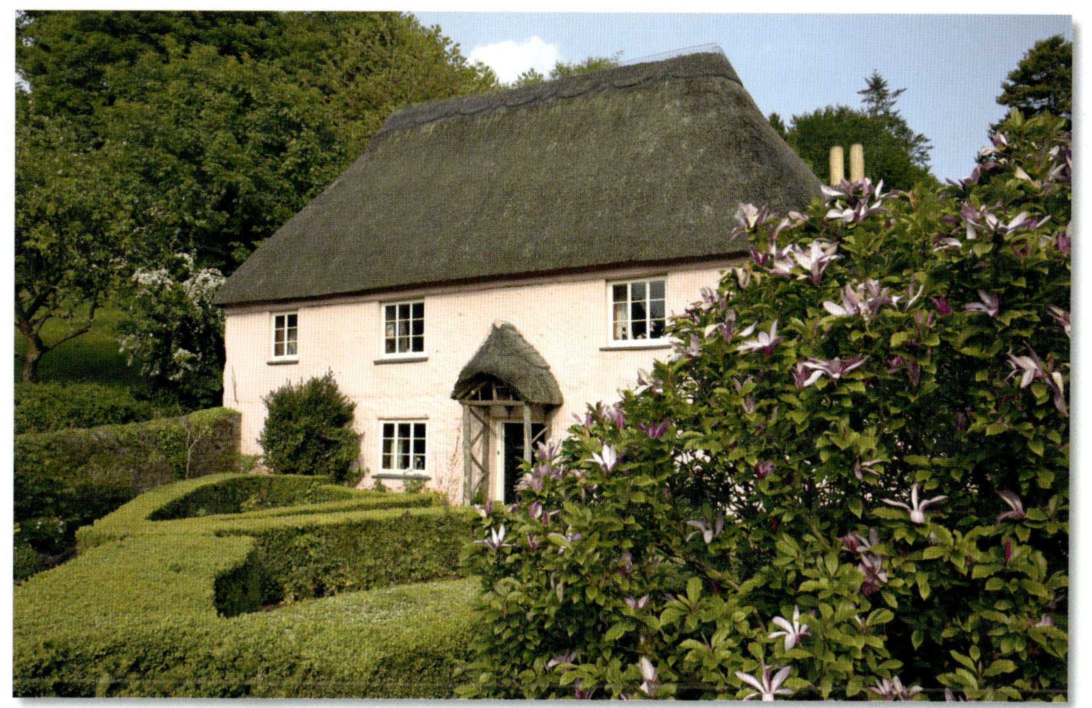

ROSE COTTAGE at Cockington Forge

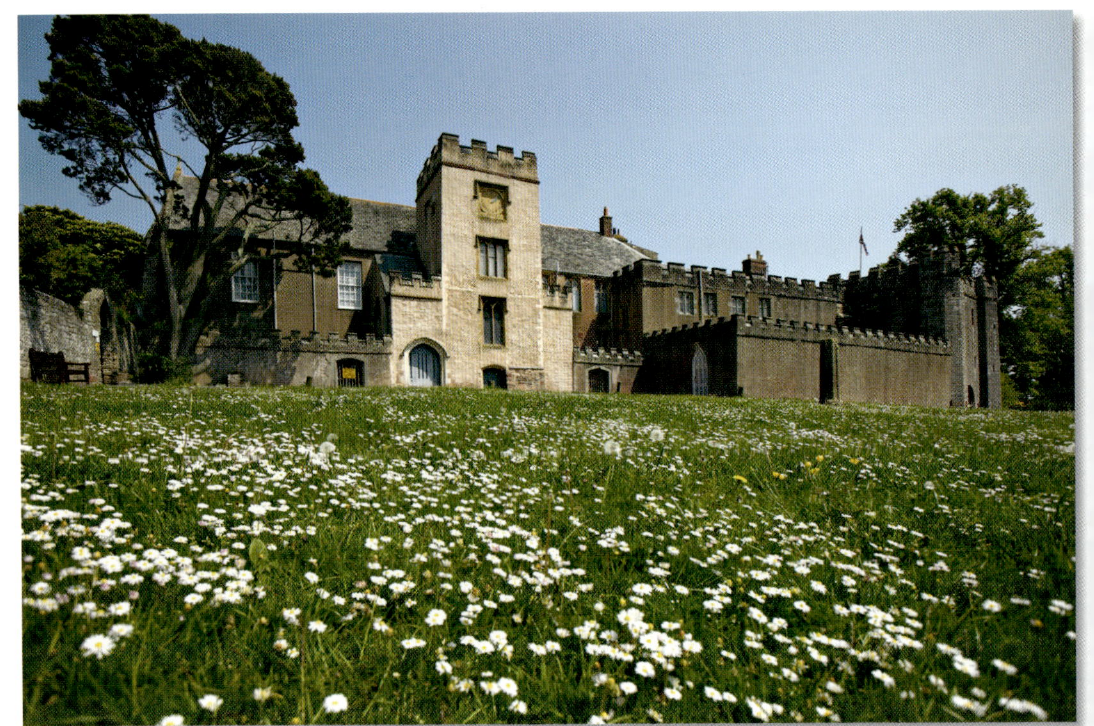

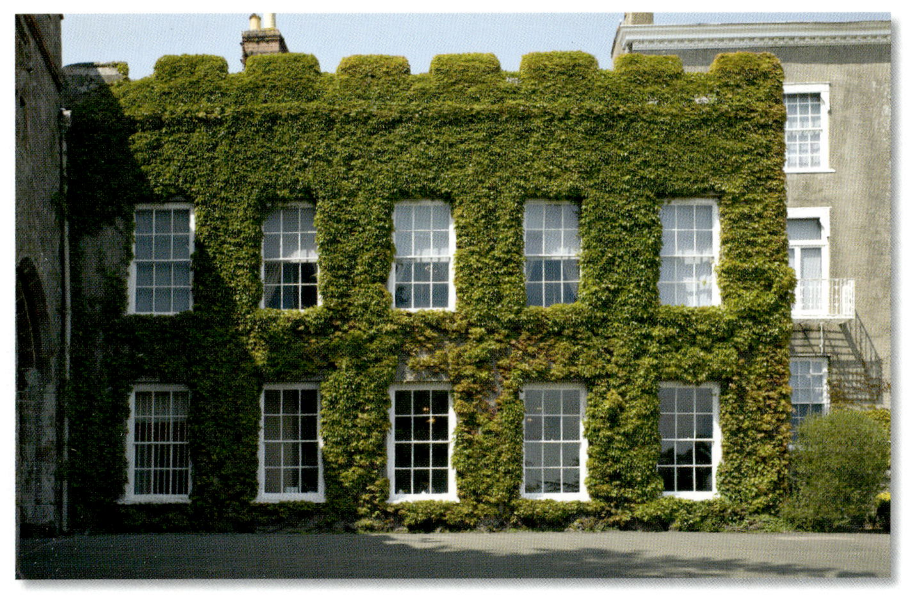

TORRE ABBEY was formed as a monastery in 1196 and converted into a home after the Dissolution of the Monasteries.

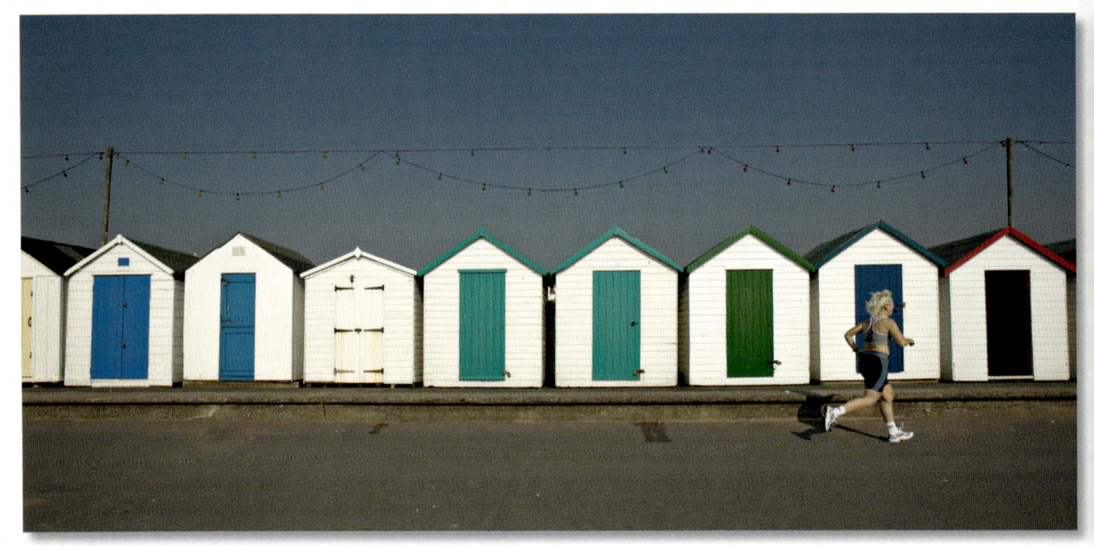

PAIGNTON Beachhuts

OLDWAY MANSION was built by the Singers, of sewing machine fame, in French Italianate style.

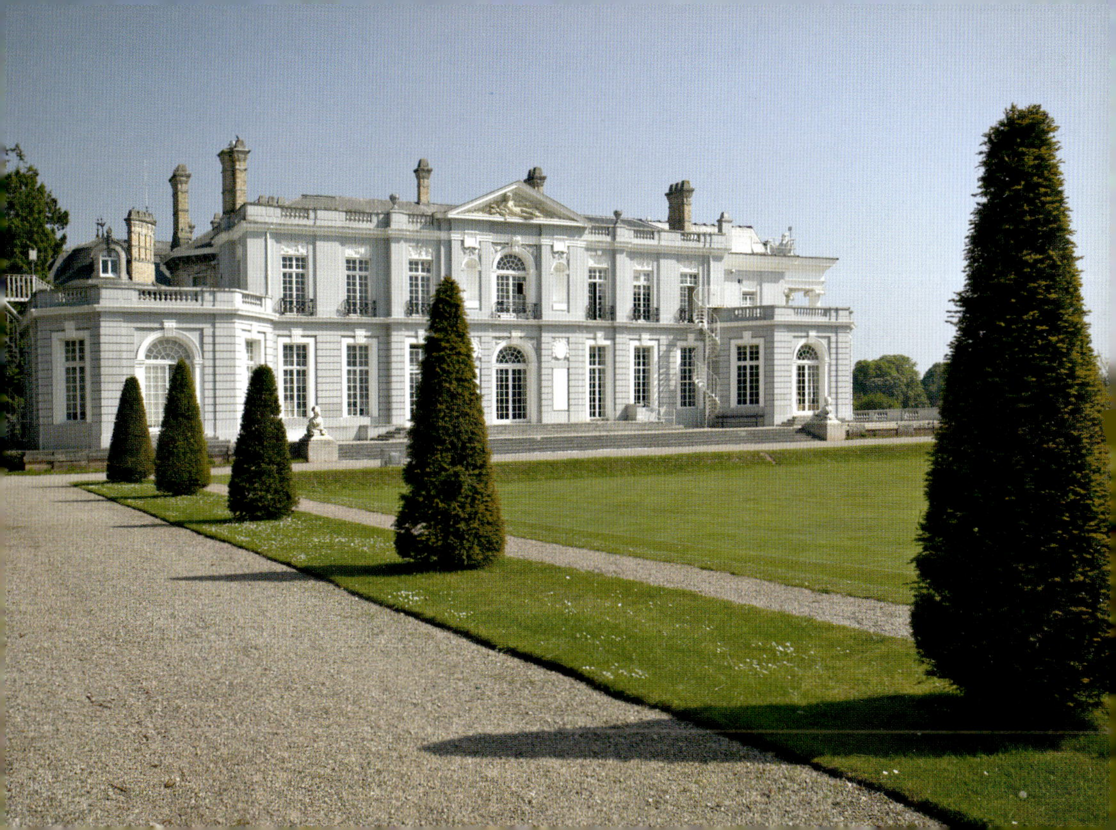

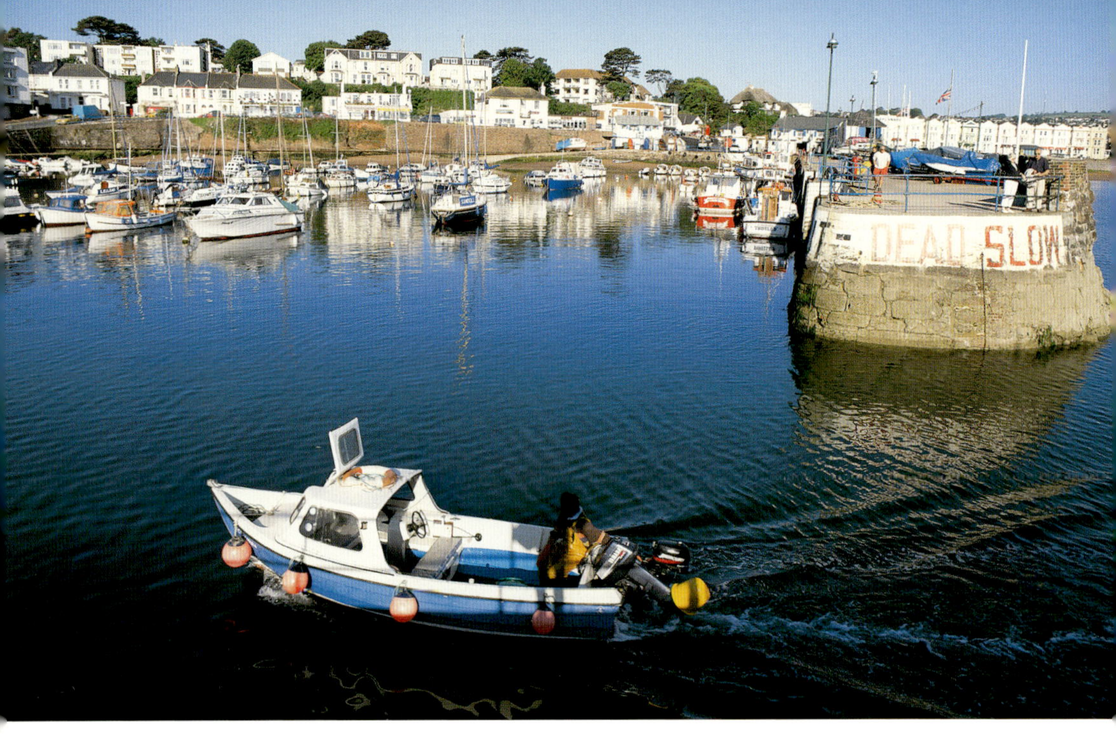

A small boat enters PAIGNTON HARBOUR

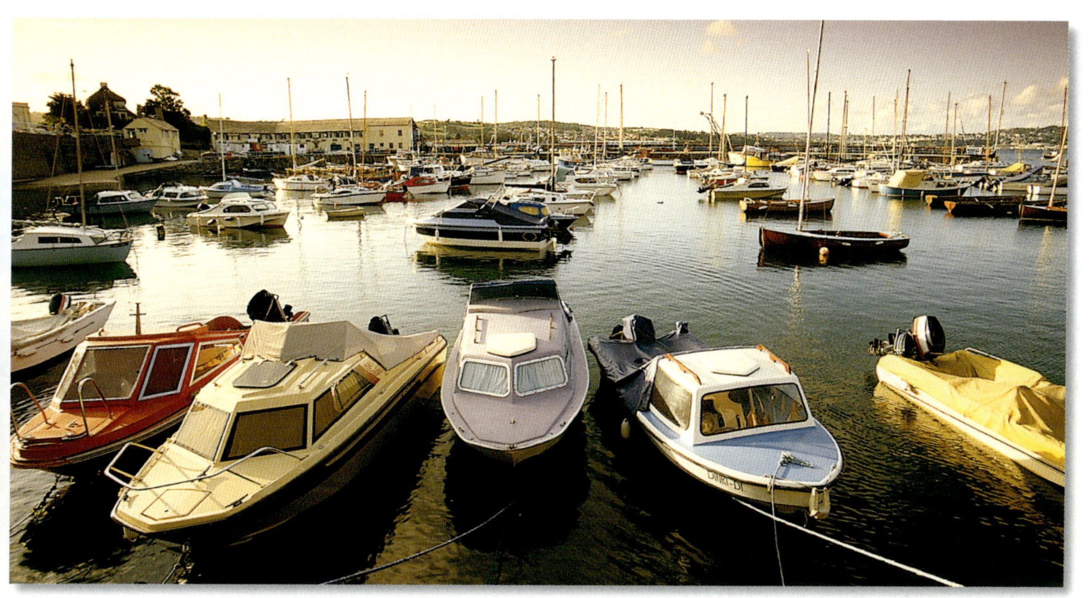

PAIGNTON HARBOUR

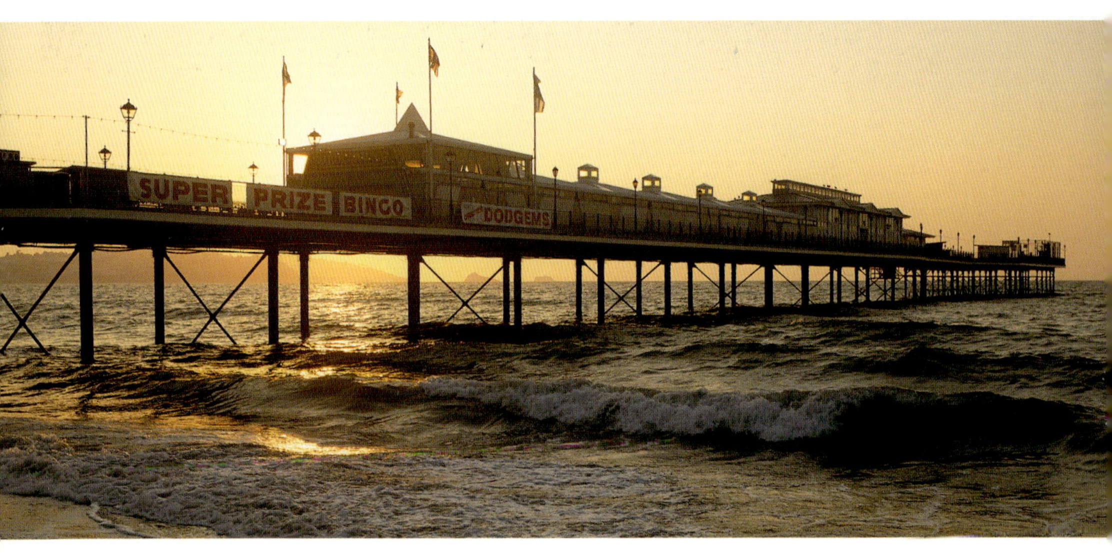

Sunrise at PAIGNTON PIER

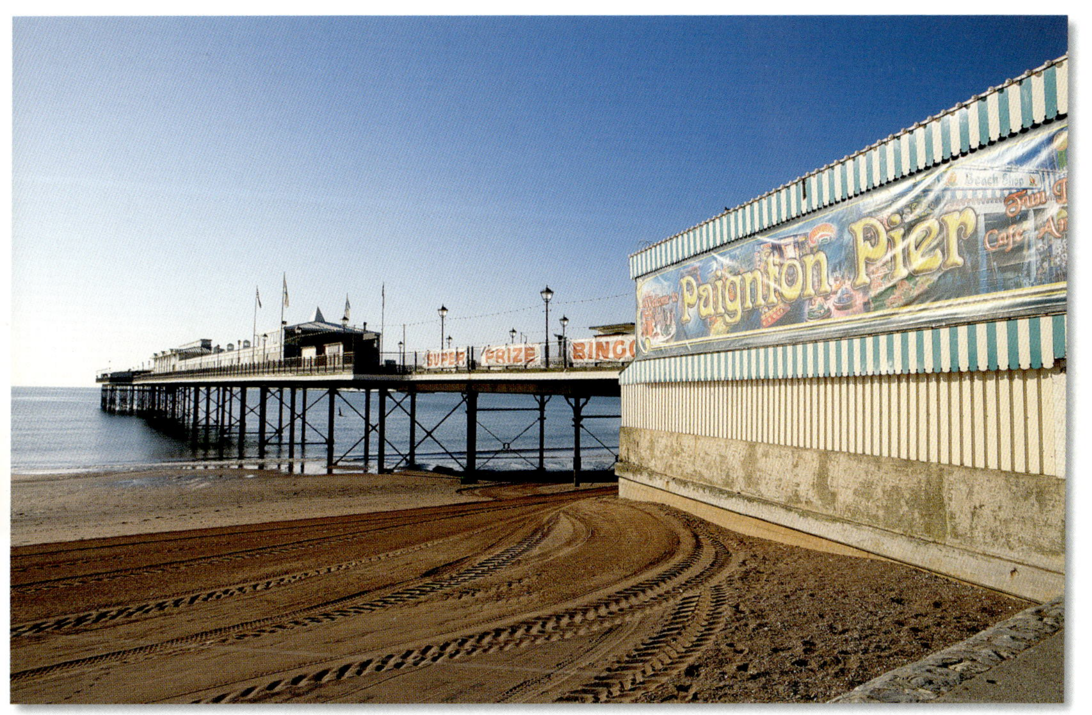

PAIGNTON PIER

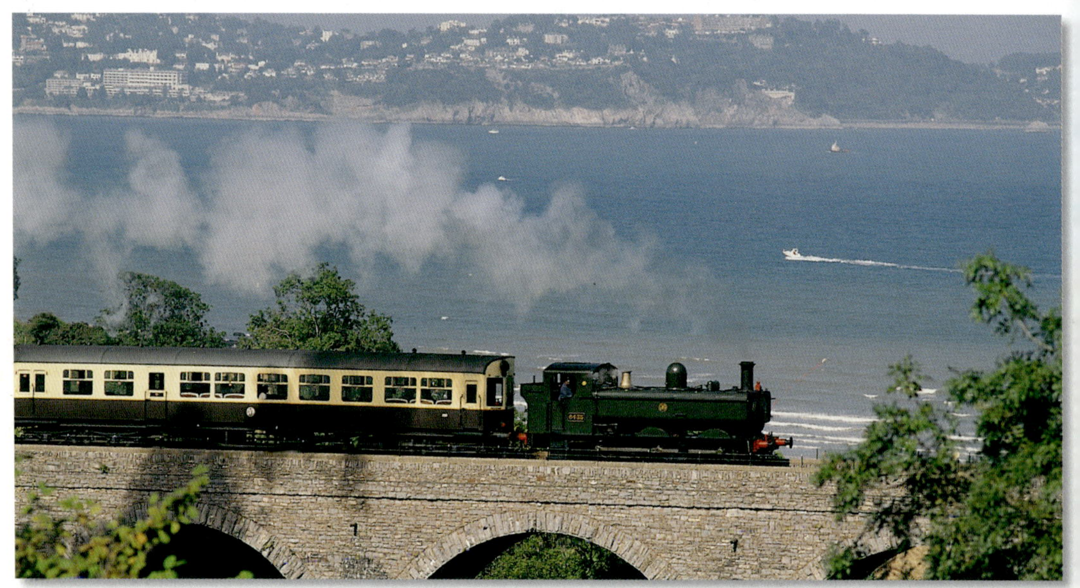

Steam Railway by the sea.

A train of the PAIGNTON & DARTMOUTH STEAM RAILWAY at Churston Station

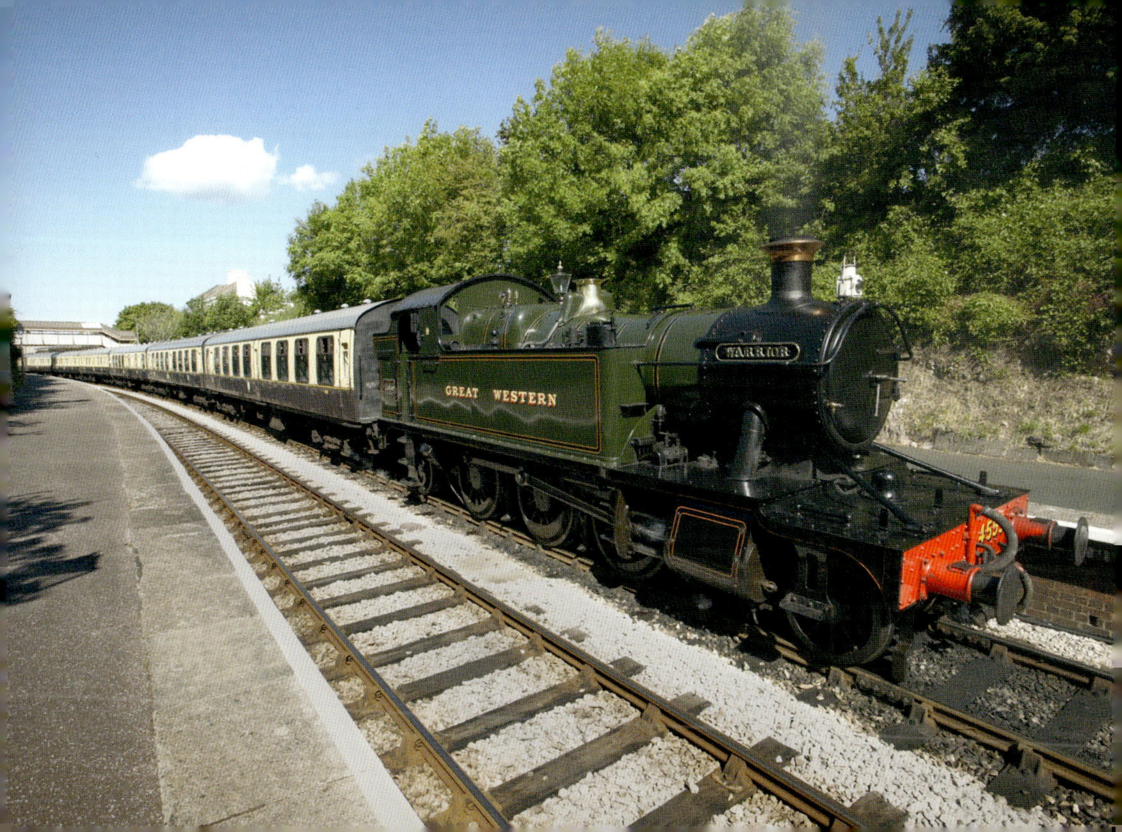
WARRIOR
GREAT WESTERN

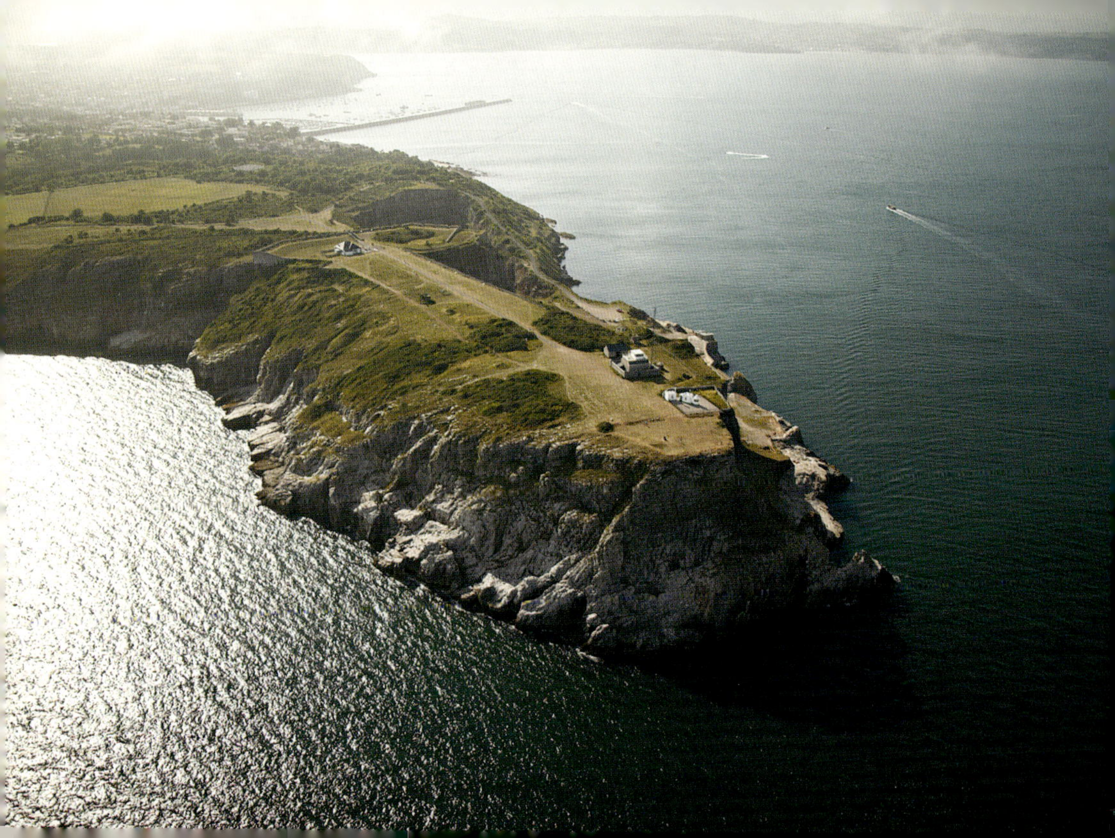

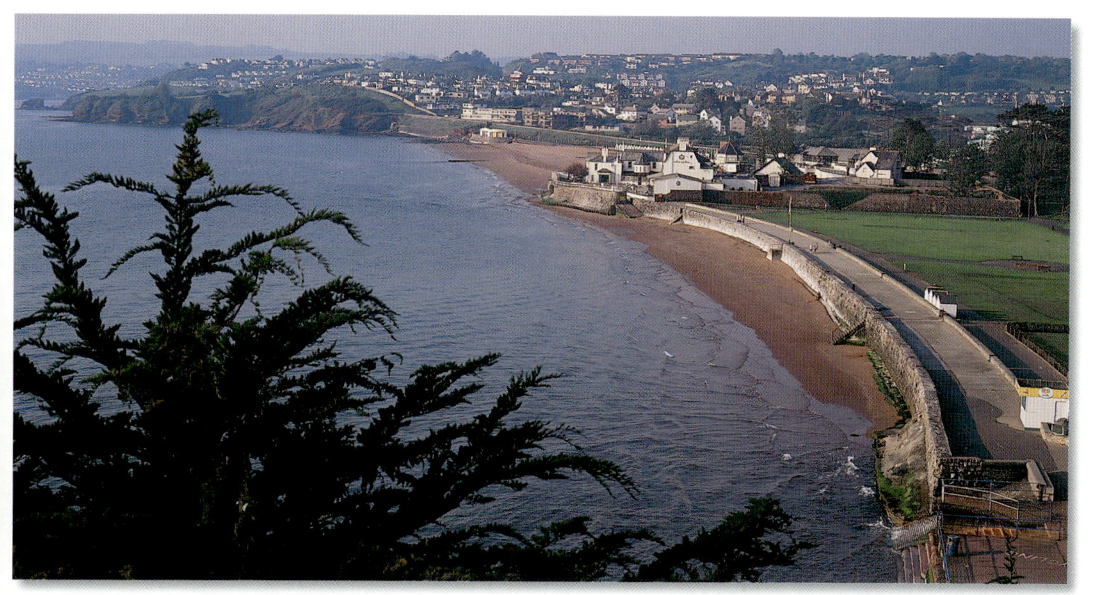

GOODRINGTON SANDS

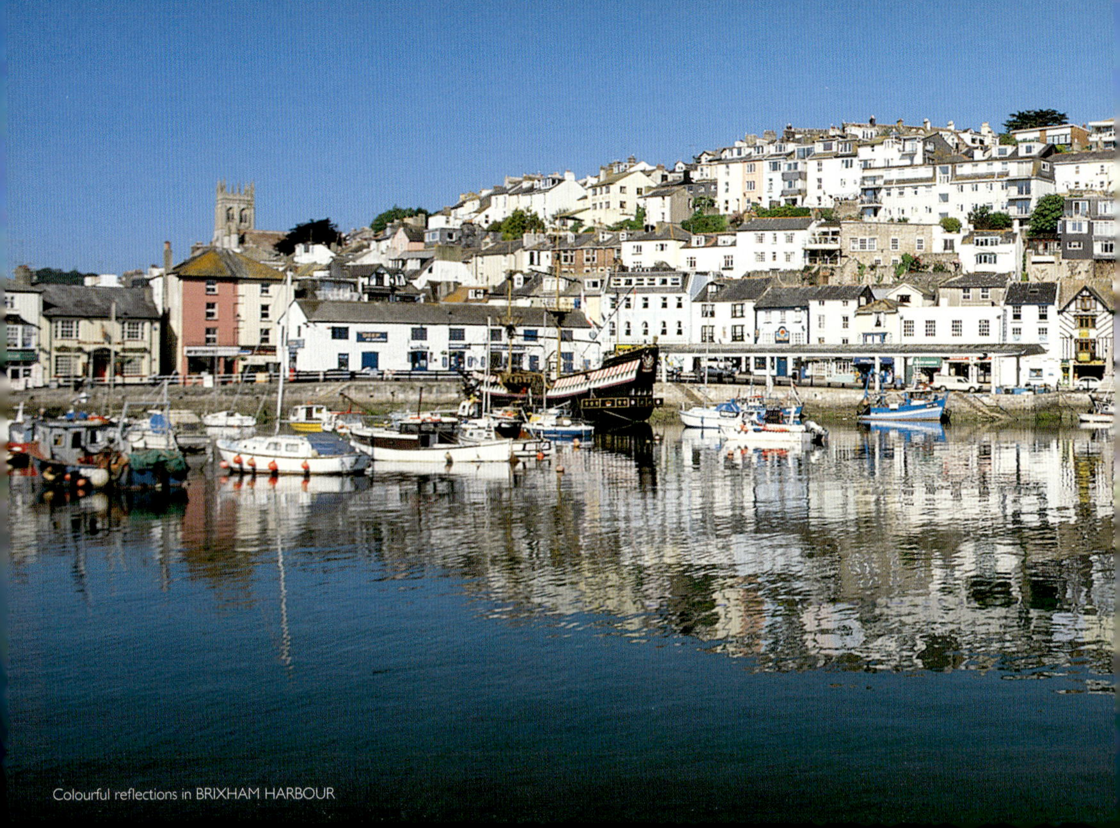

Colourful reflections in BRIXHAM HARBOUR

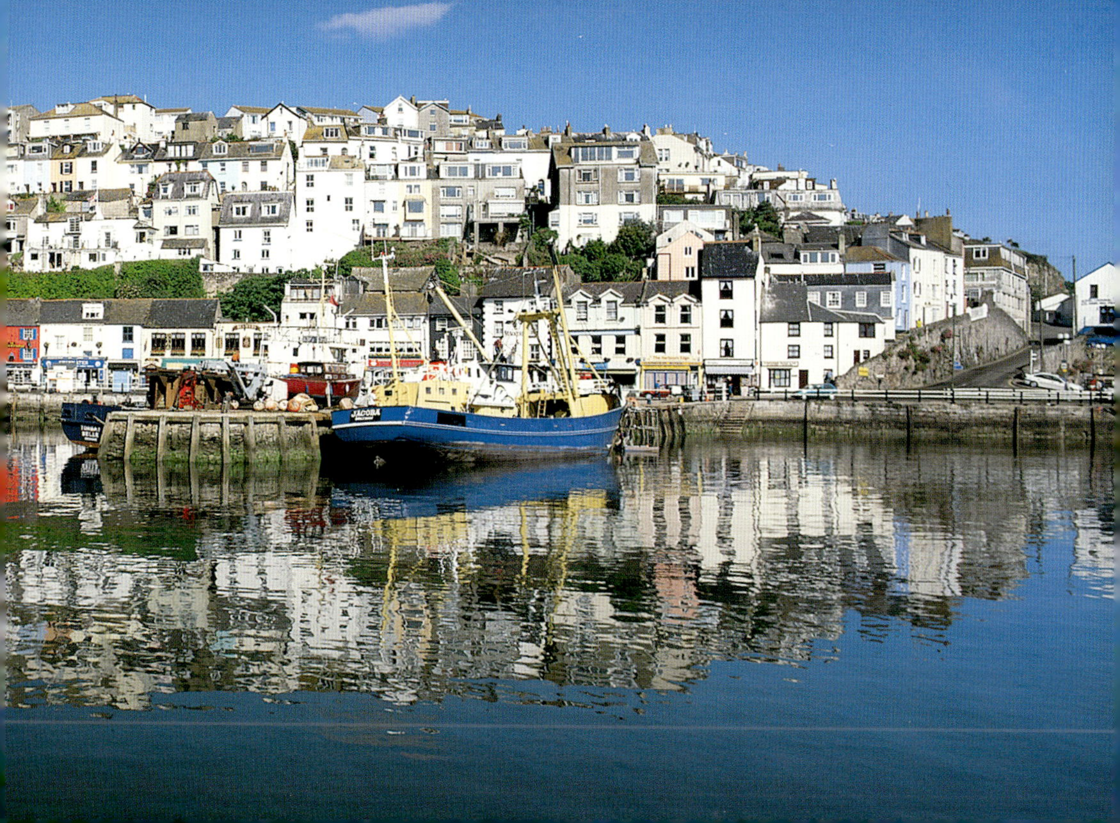
JACOBA

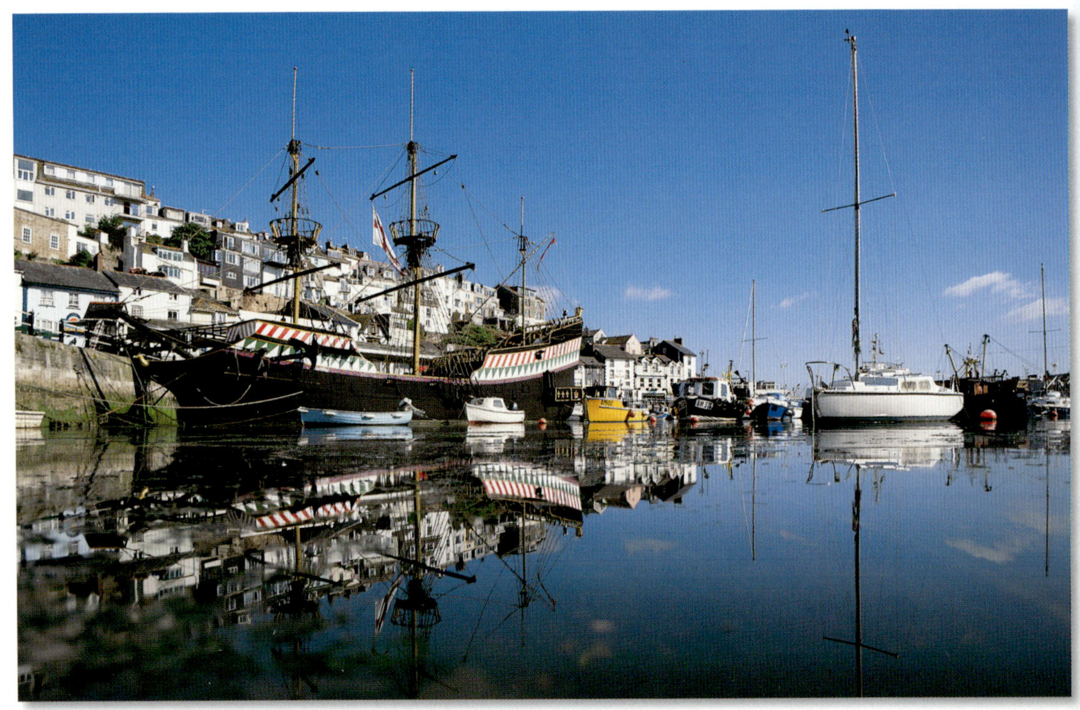

Reflections in Brixham Harbour showing the replica of the GOLDEN HIND

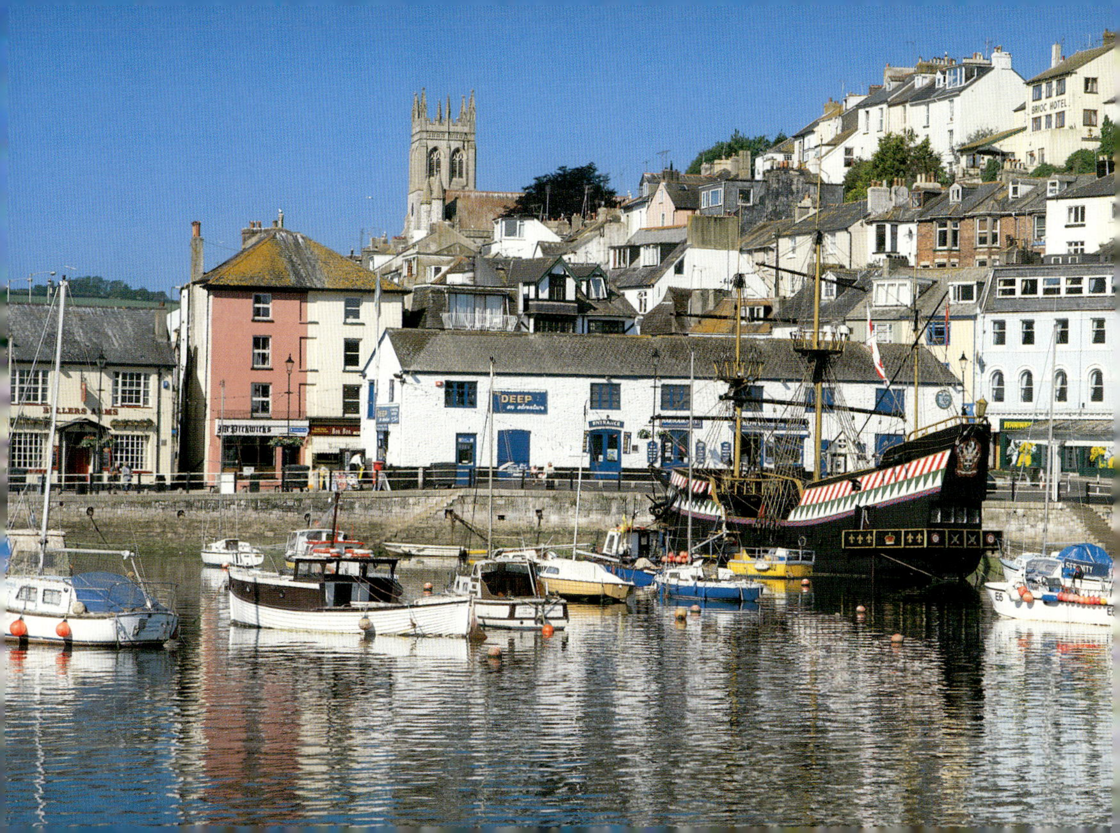
BRIOC HOTEL
DEEP
on adventure
Mr Pickwicks

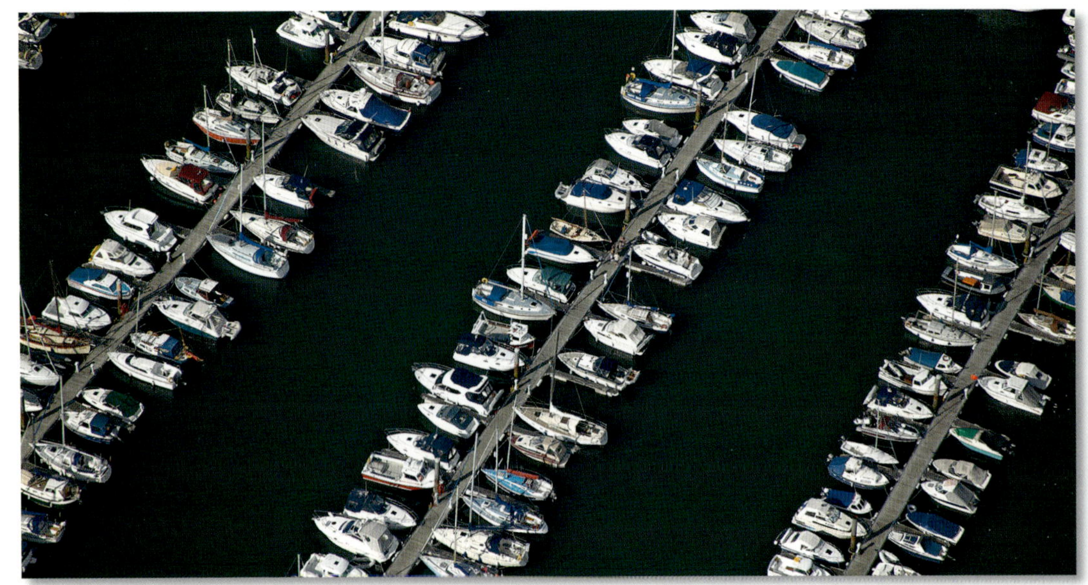

An aerial view of BRIXHAM Marina

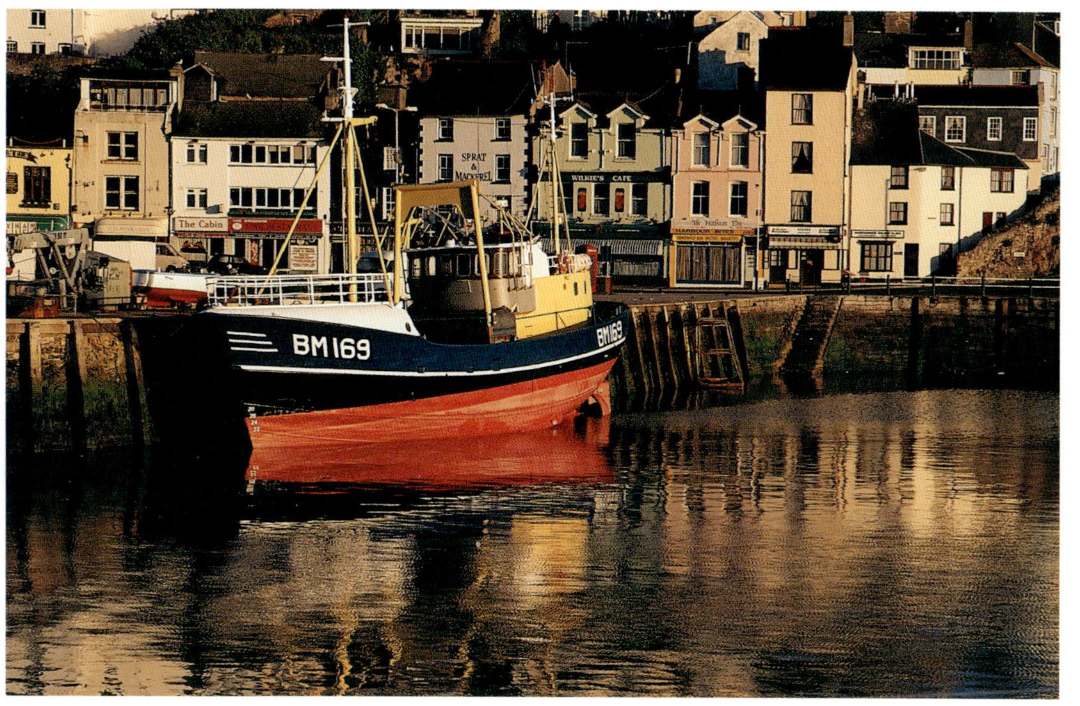

Dawn reveals a Brixham Trawler in the old harbour.

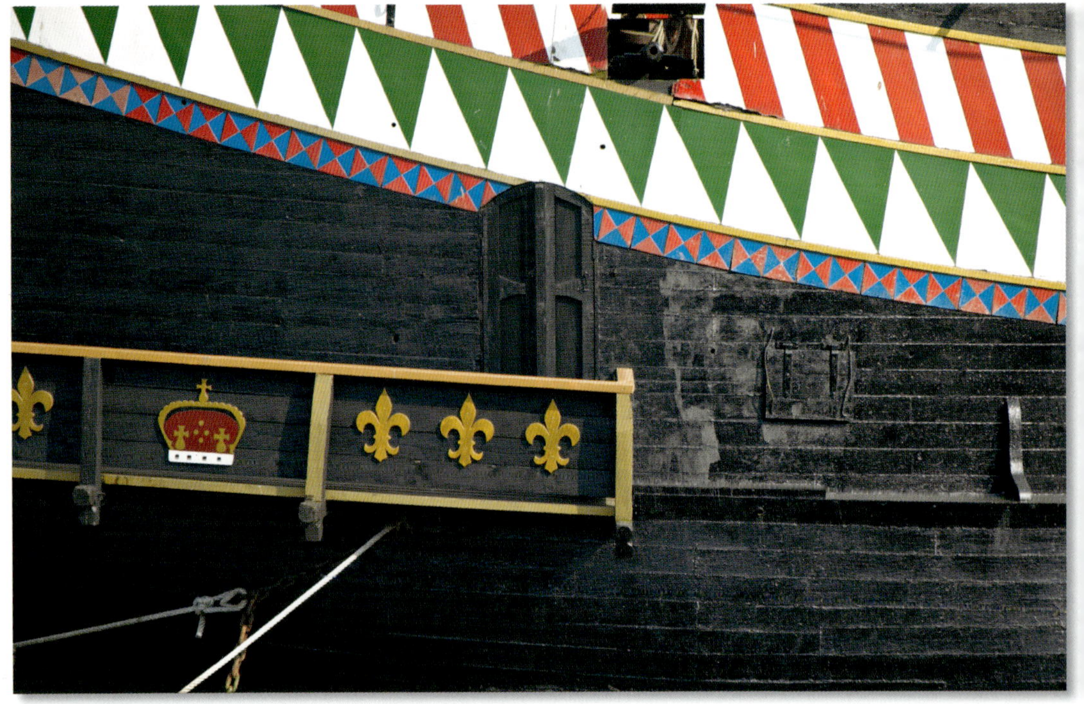

A detail of the GOLDEN HIND replica

Prince William of Orange landed at Brixham in 1688

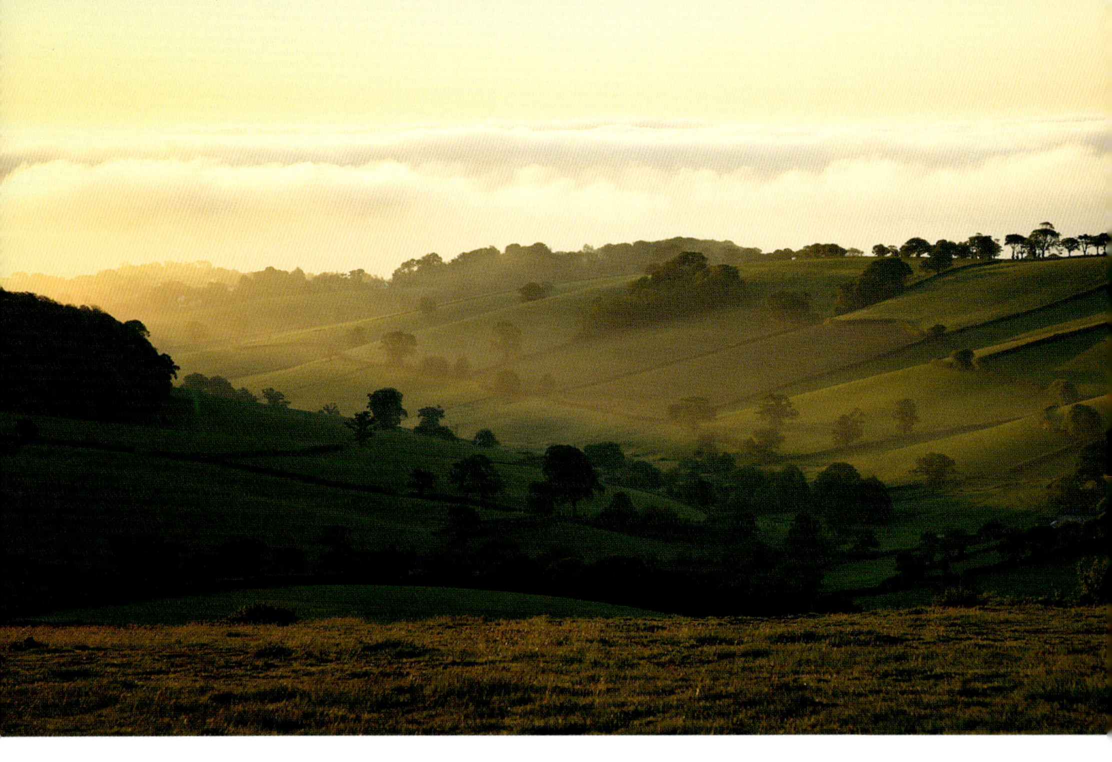

The early morning sun fills a valley above DAWLISH with light.

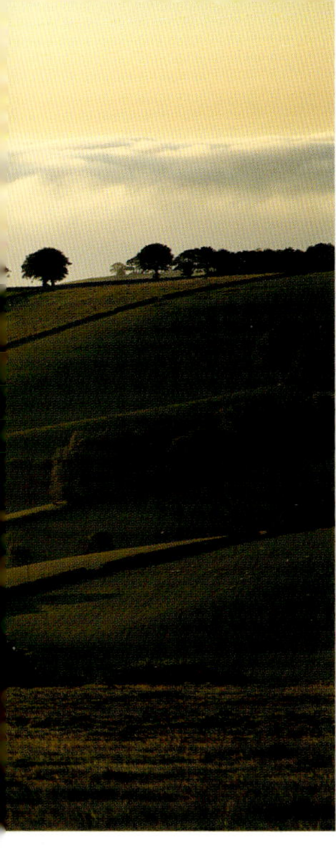

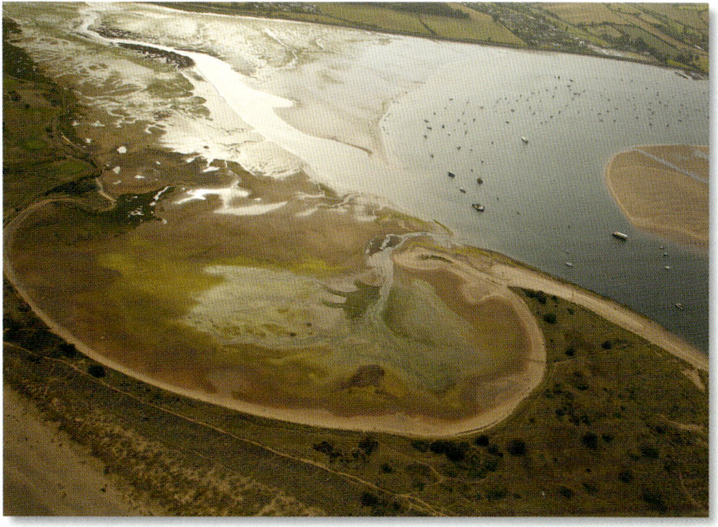

The sand flats of DAWLISH WARREN from the air.

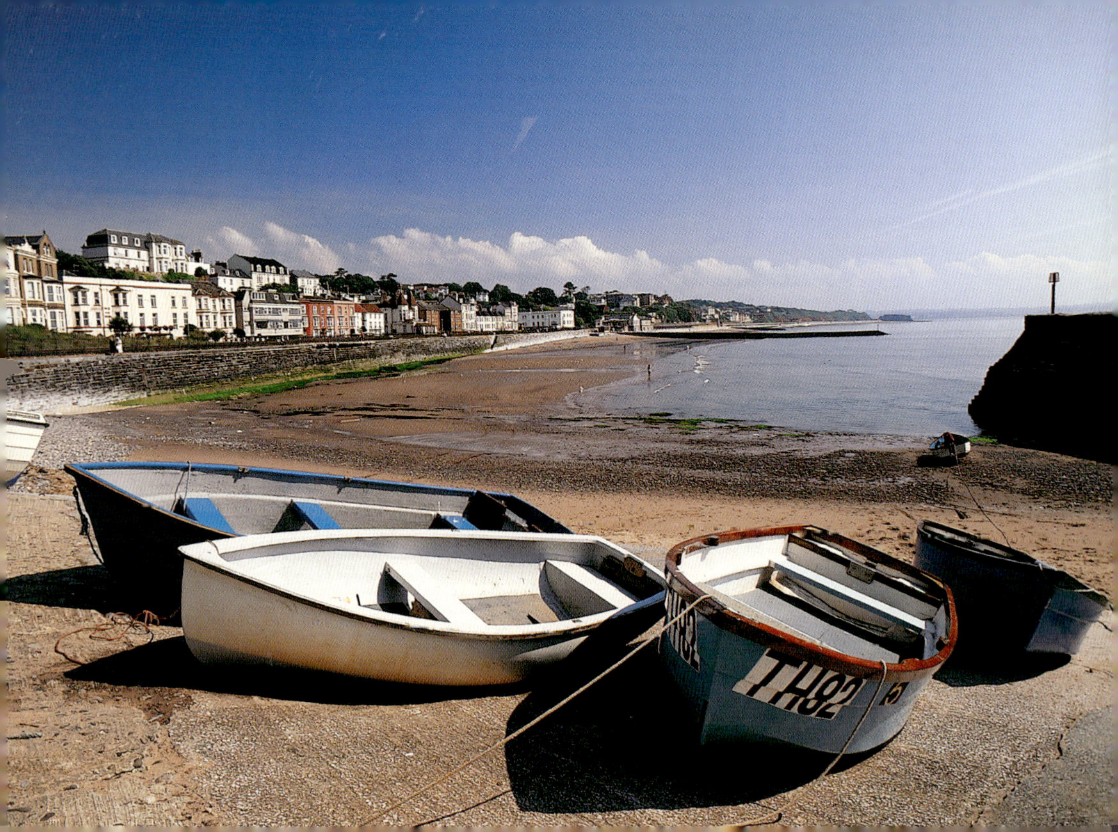
TH82

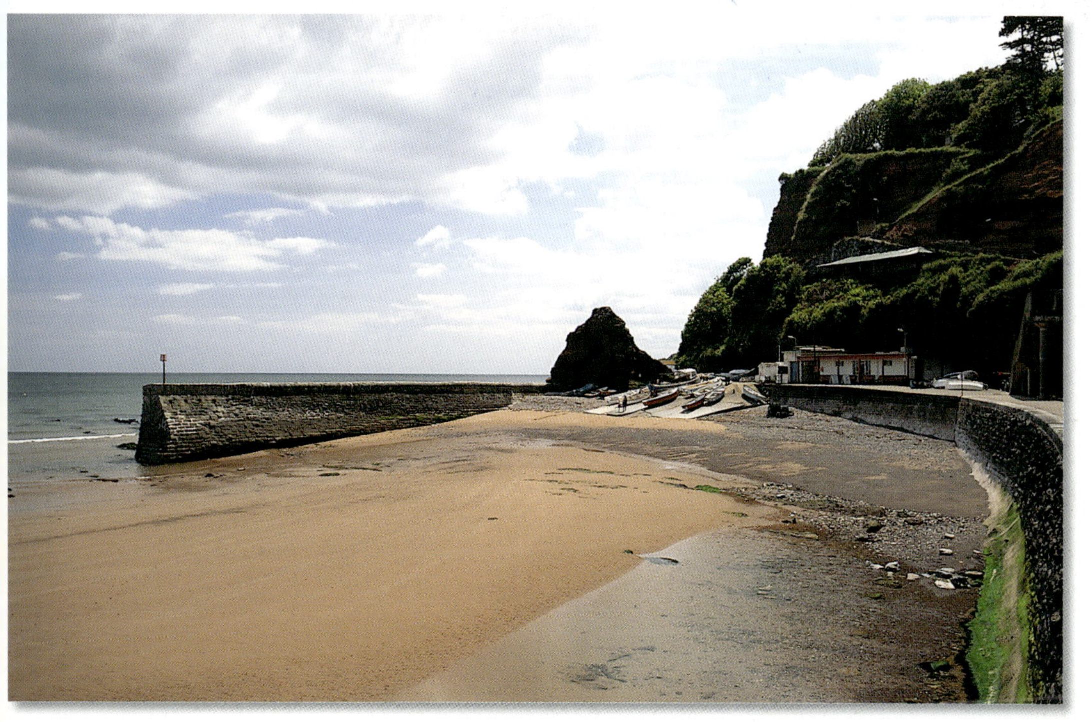

The small sheltered harbour at DAWLISH

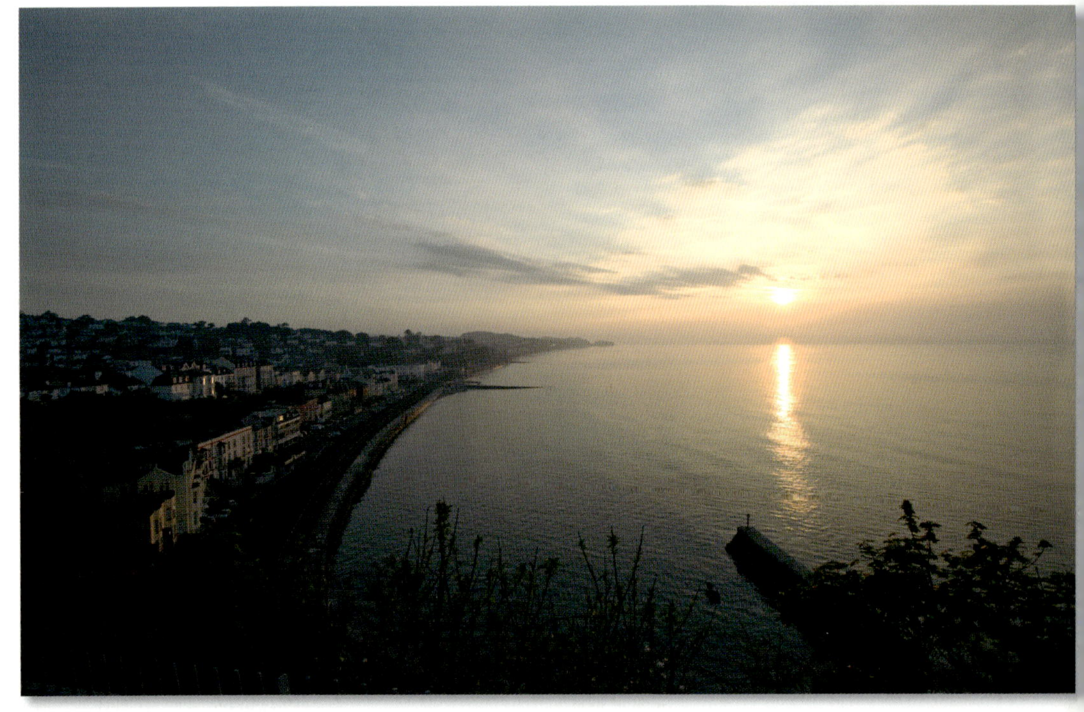

The sun rises over DAWLISH

Early morning reflections at COCKWOOD Harbour

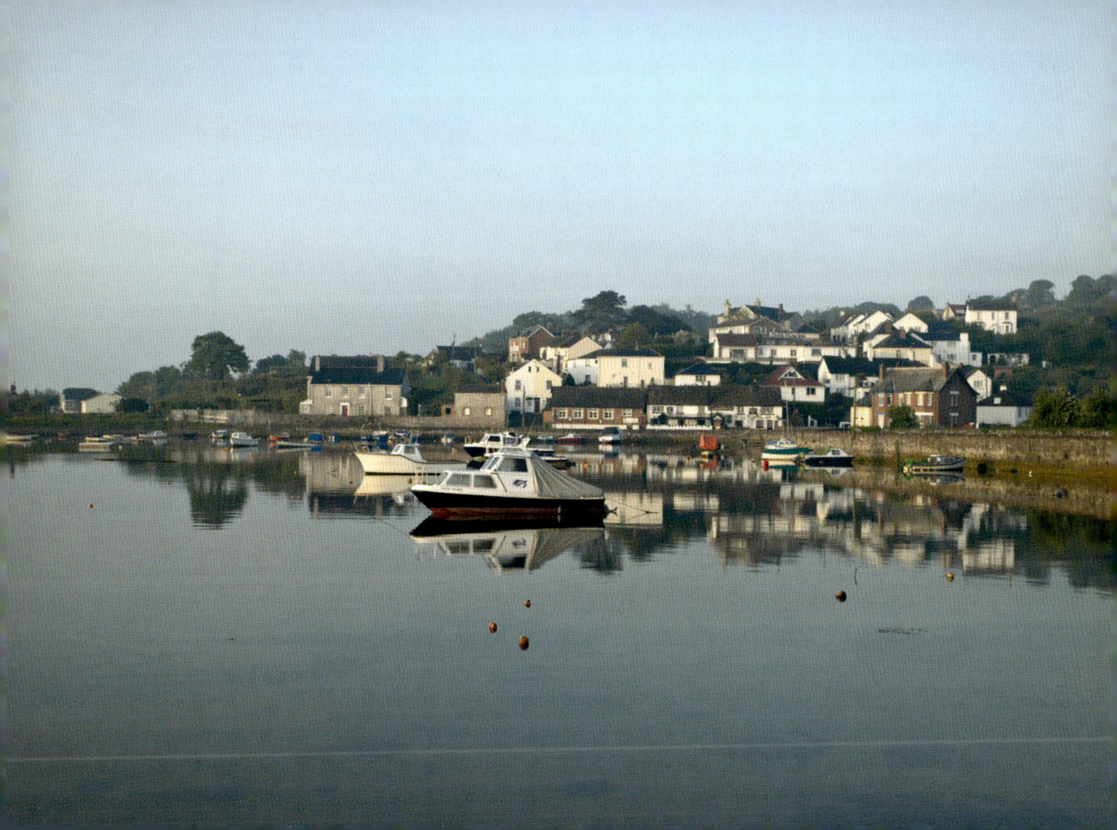

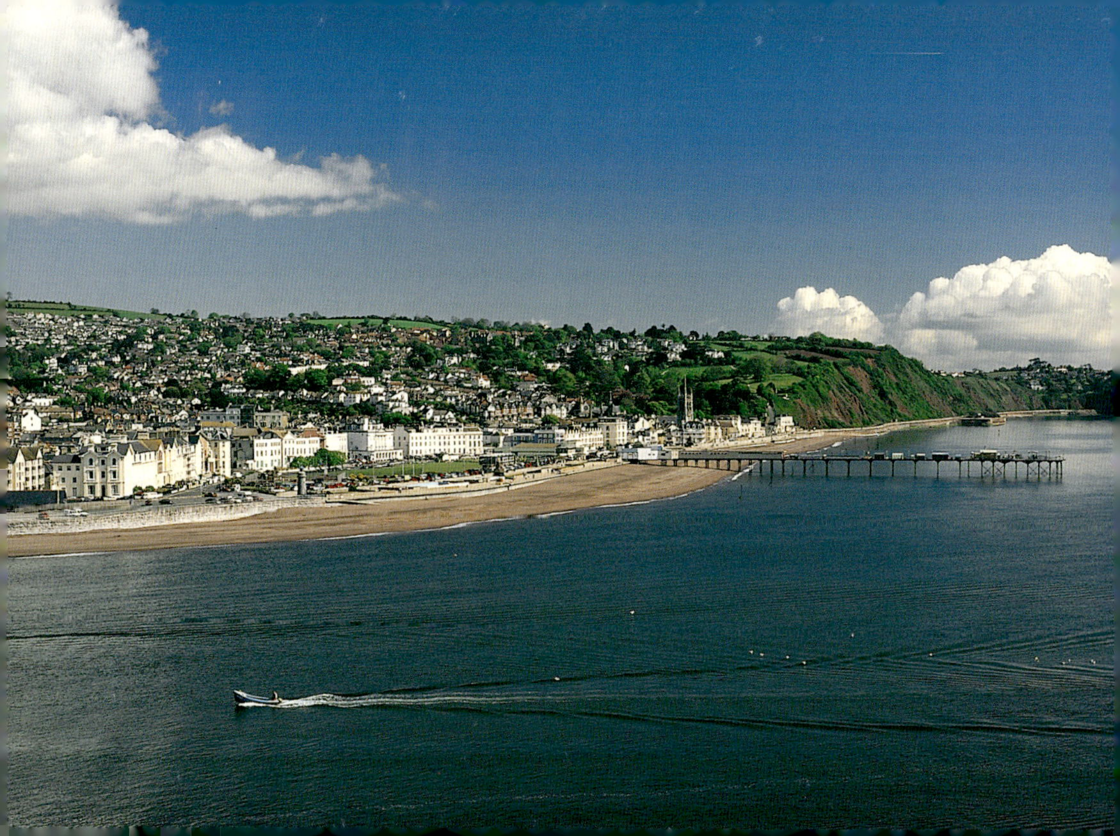

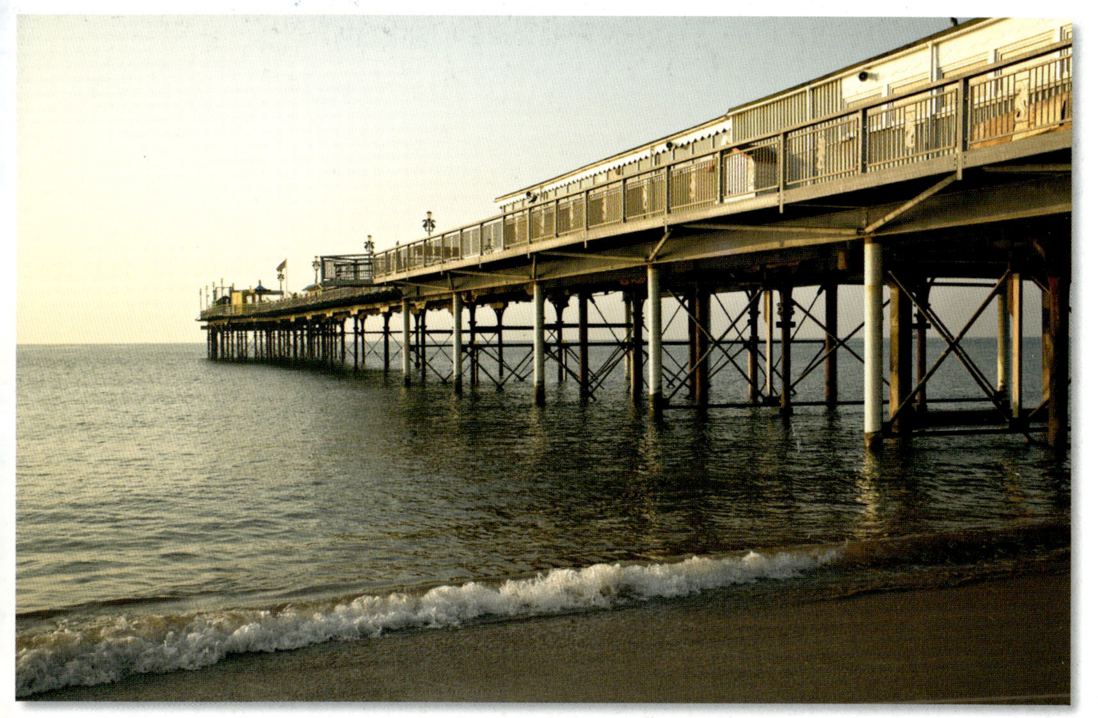

TEIGNMOUTH with its pier and seafront hotels

TEIGNMOUTH PIER

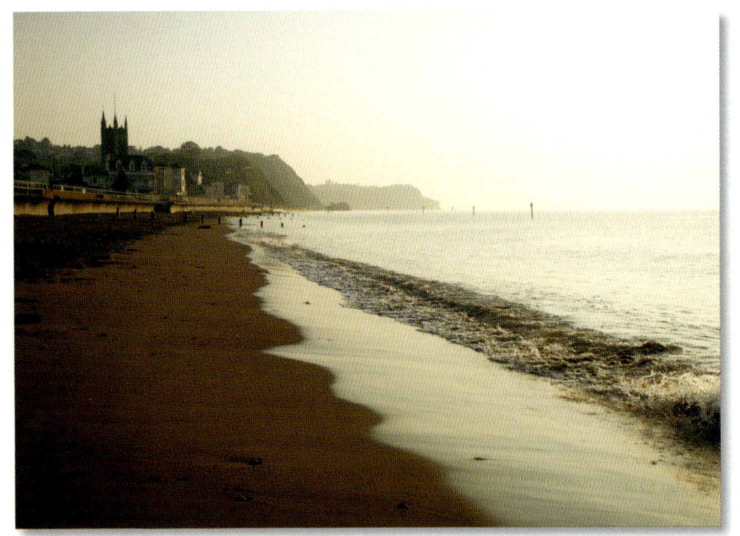

TEIGNMOUTH BEACH

TEIGNMOUTH and The Ness from the air

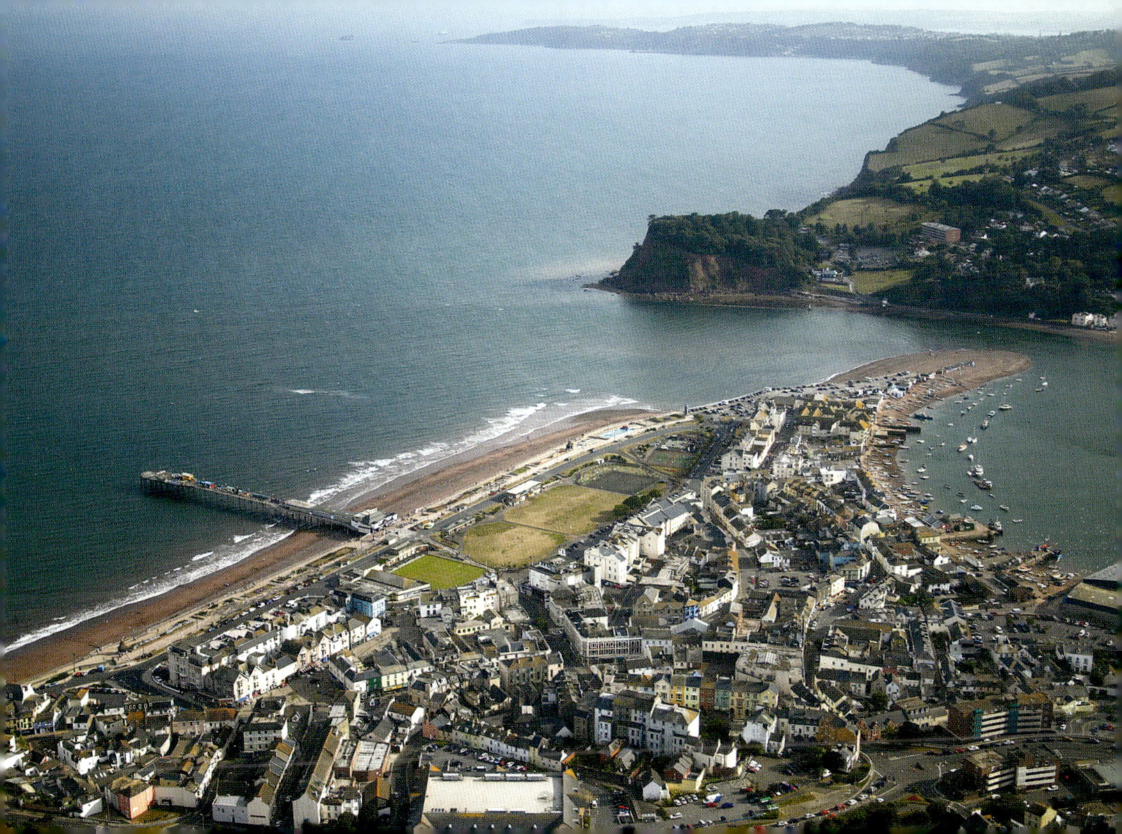

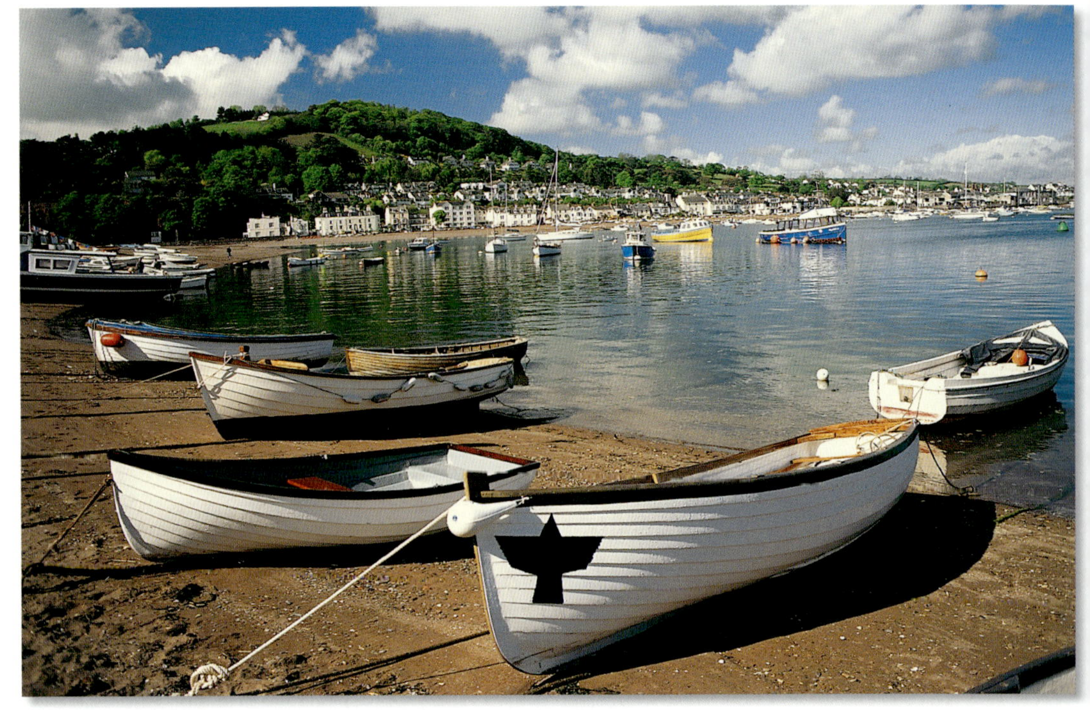

Boats on the beach at TEIGNMOUTH with Shaldon in the distance

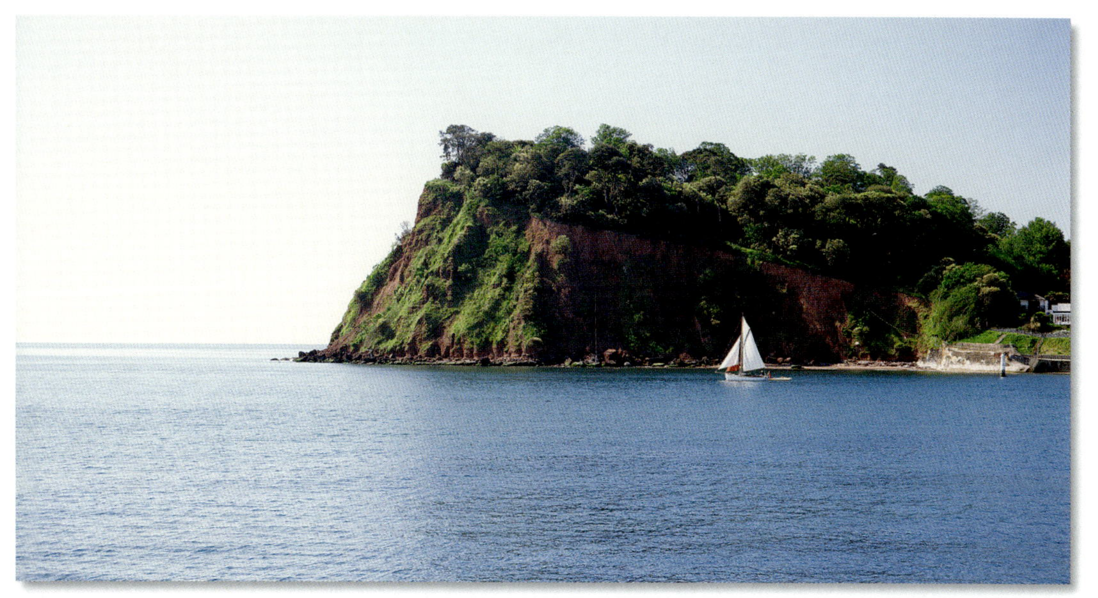

THE NESS is a distinctive outcrop of red Devon rock

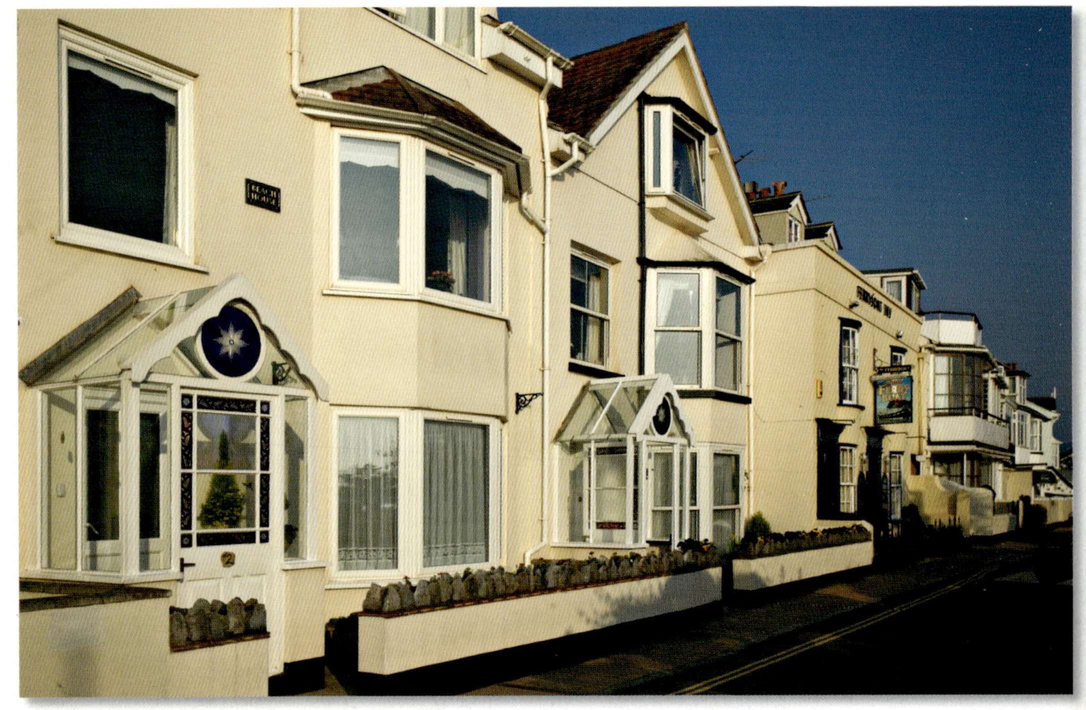

SHALDON beach with boats on the shore and The Ness in the background

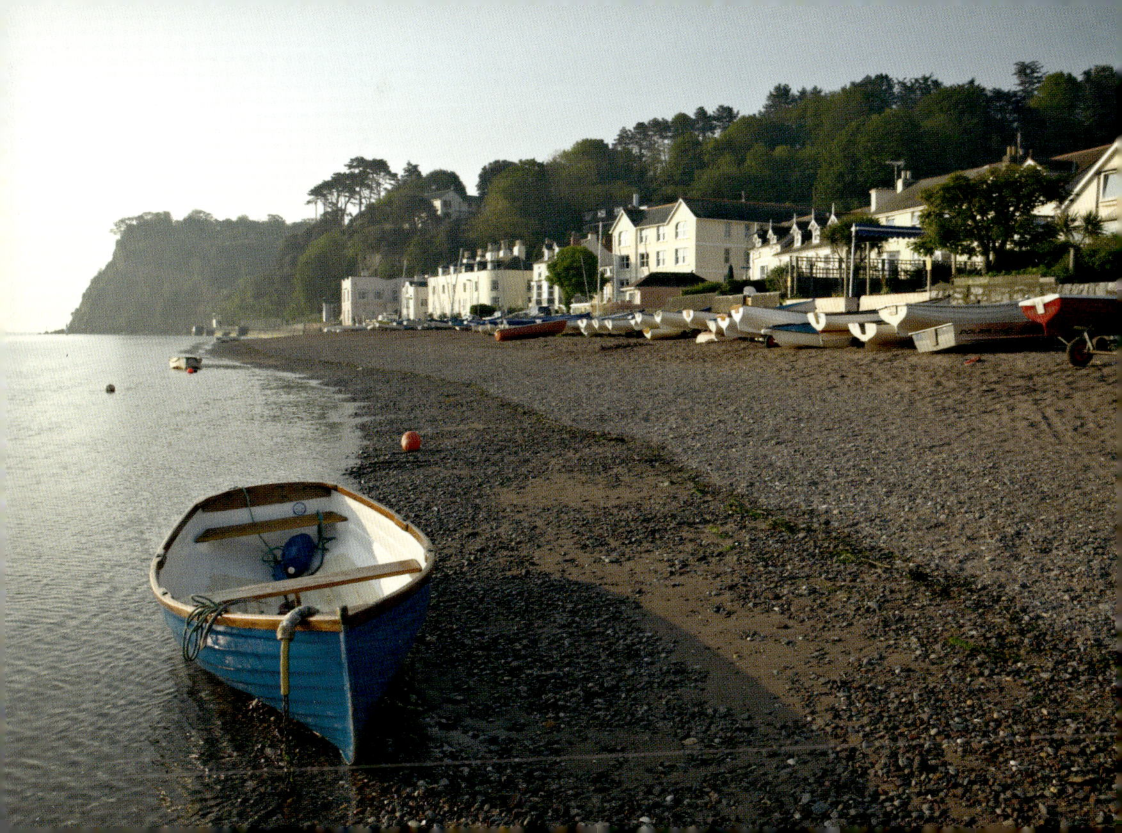

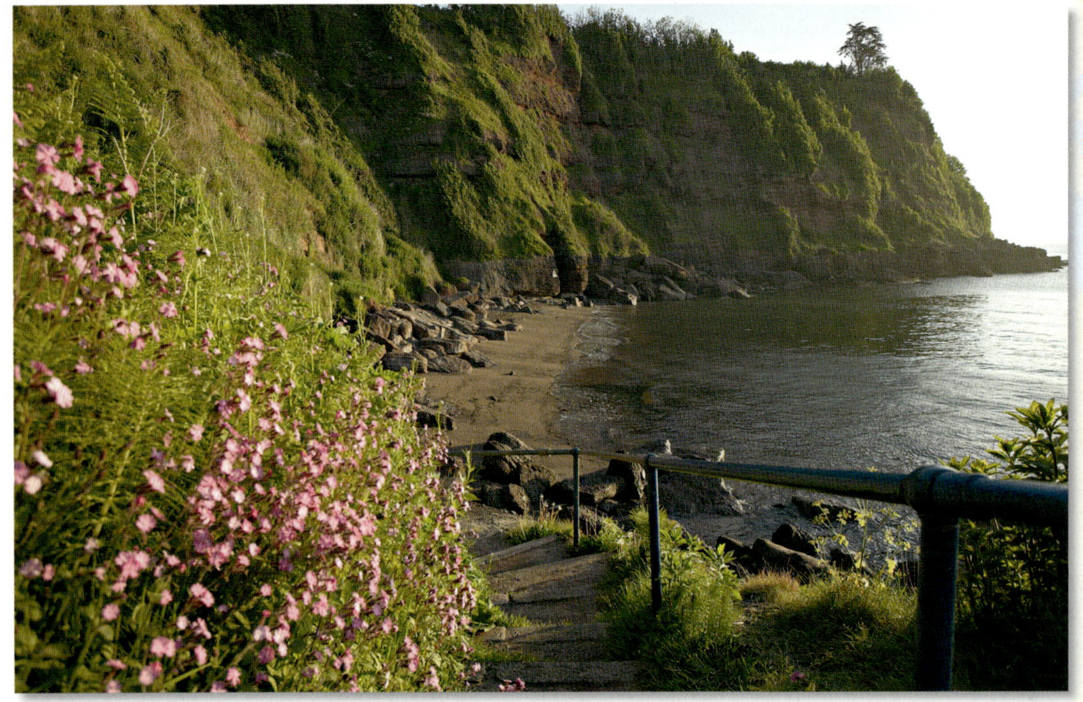

MAIDENCOMBE BEACH with its distinctive red cliffs and sand

The church at ST MARYCHURCH

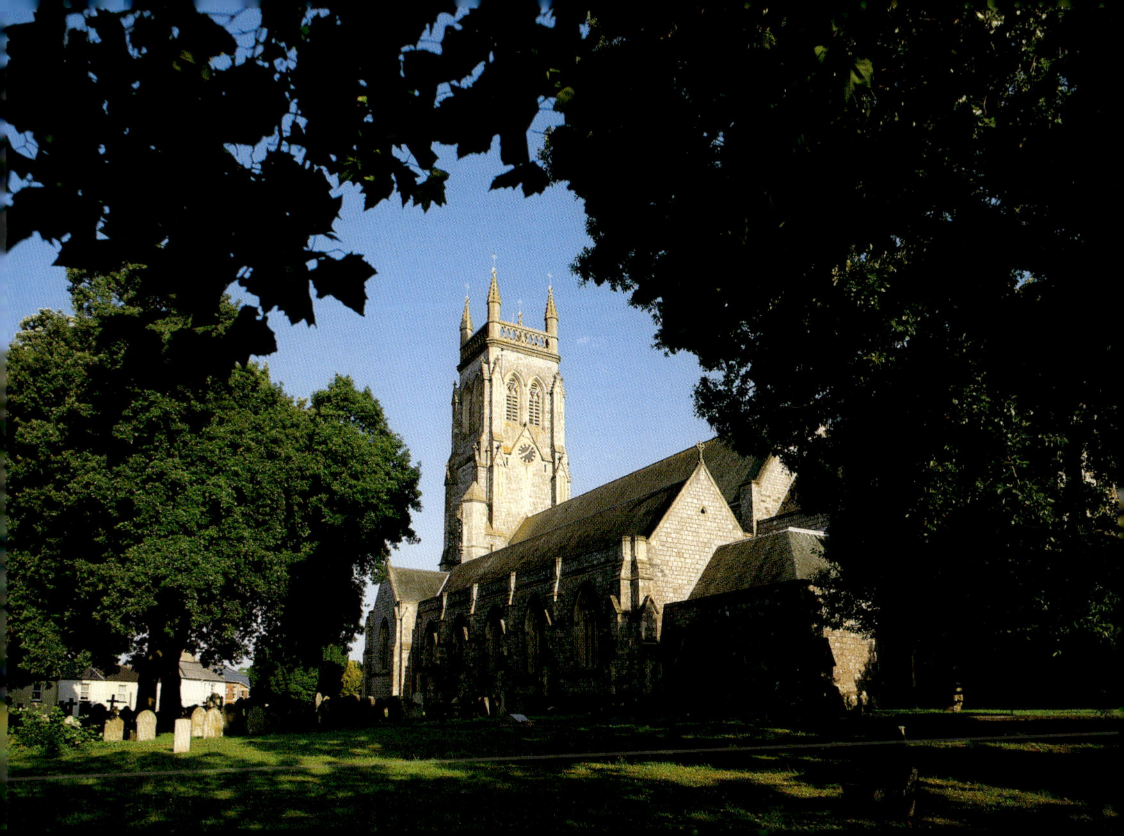

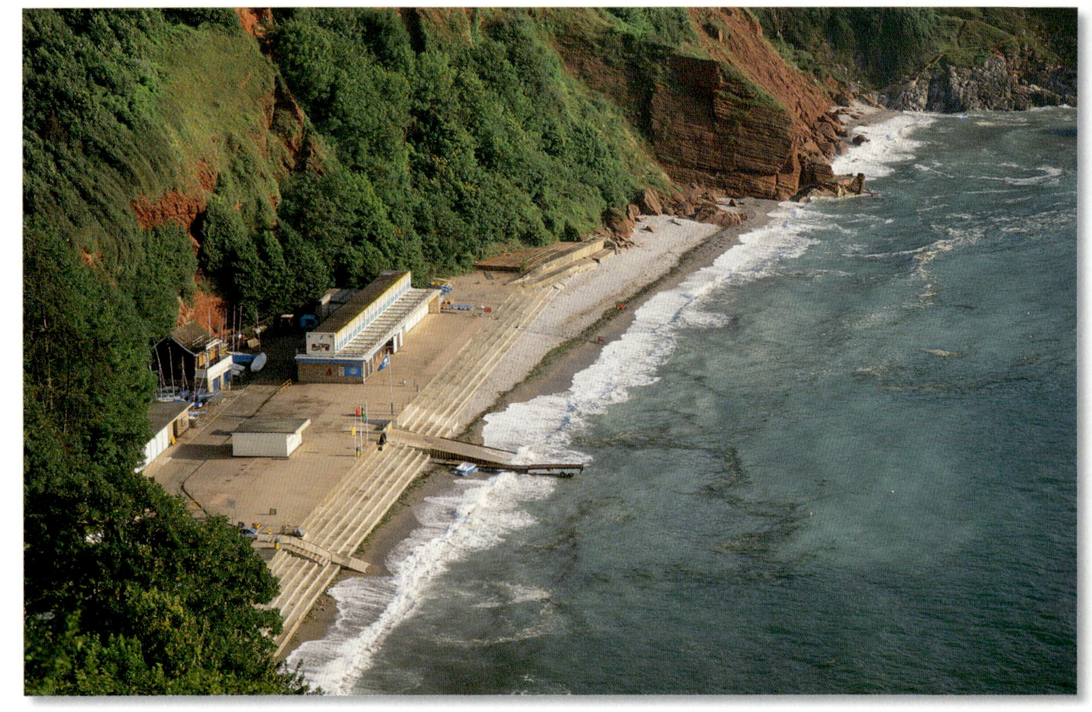

ODDICOMBE BEACH from the Clifftop Promenade at Babbacombe

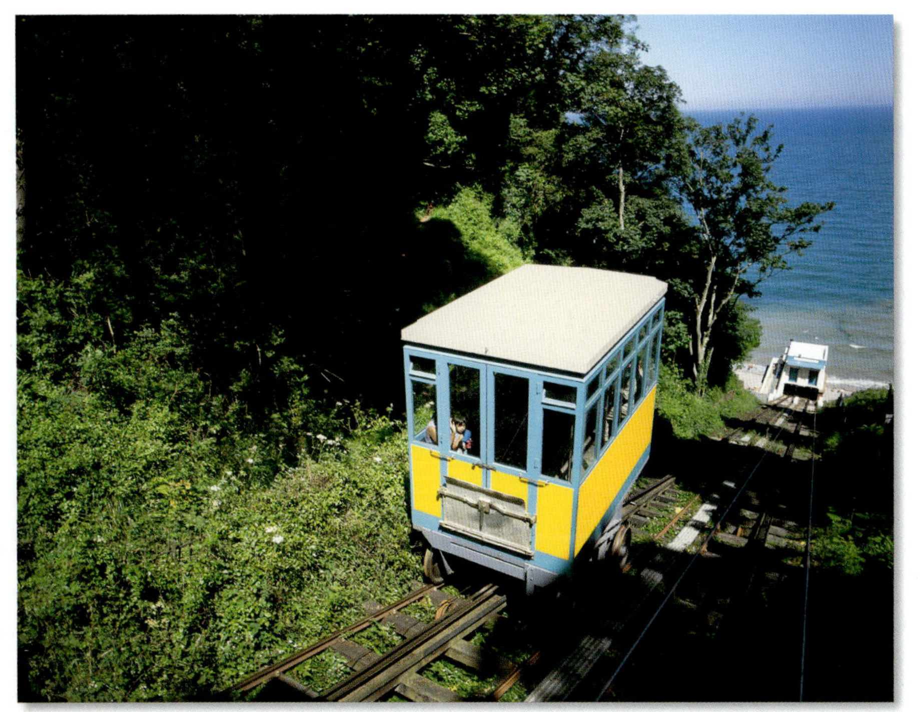

The CLIFF RAILWAY carries passengers on a gentle ride to the beach

Many thanks to:- The Paignton & Dartmouth Steam Railway for permission to photograph at Churston Station and Torbay Council for permission to photograph at Oldway Mansion and Torre Abbey.

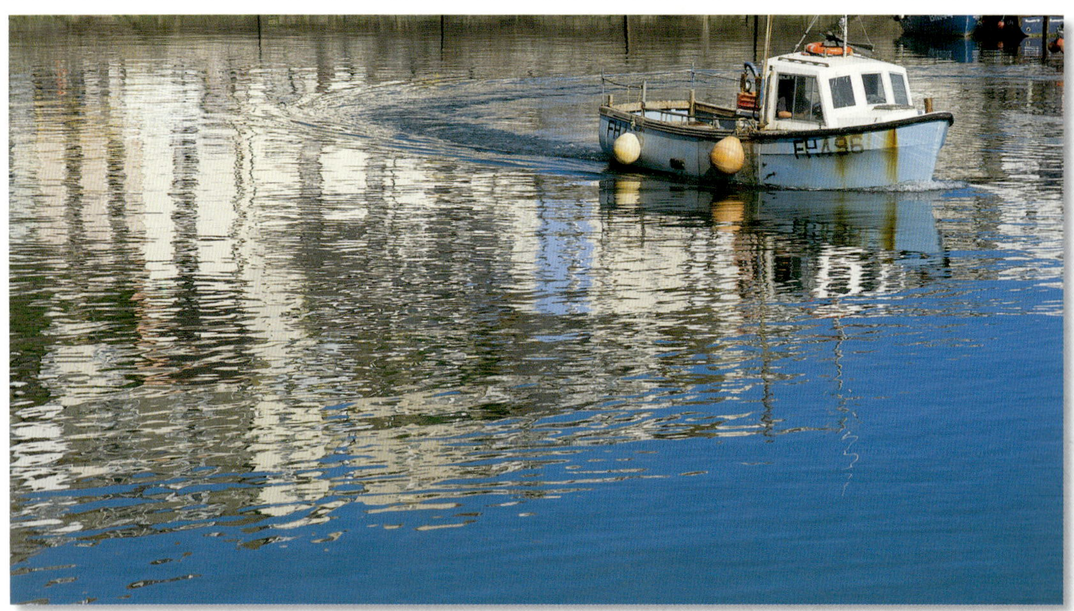

Harbour reflections in BRIXHAM

INDEX

Deckchairs on TORQUAY'S Promenade (overleaf)

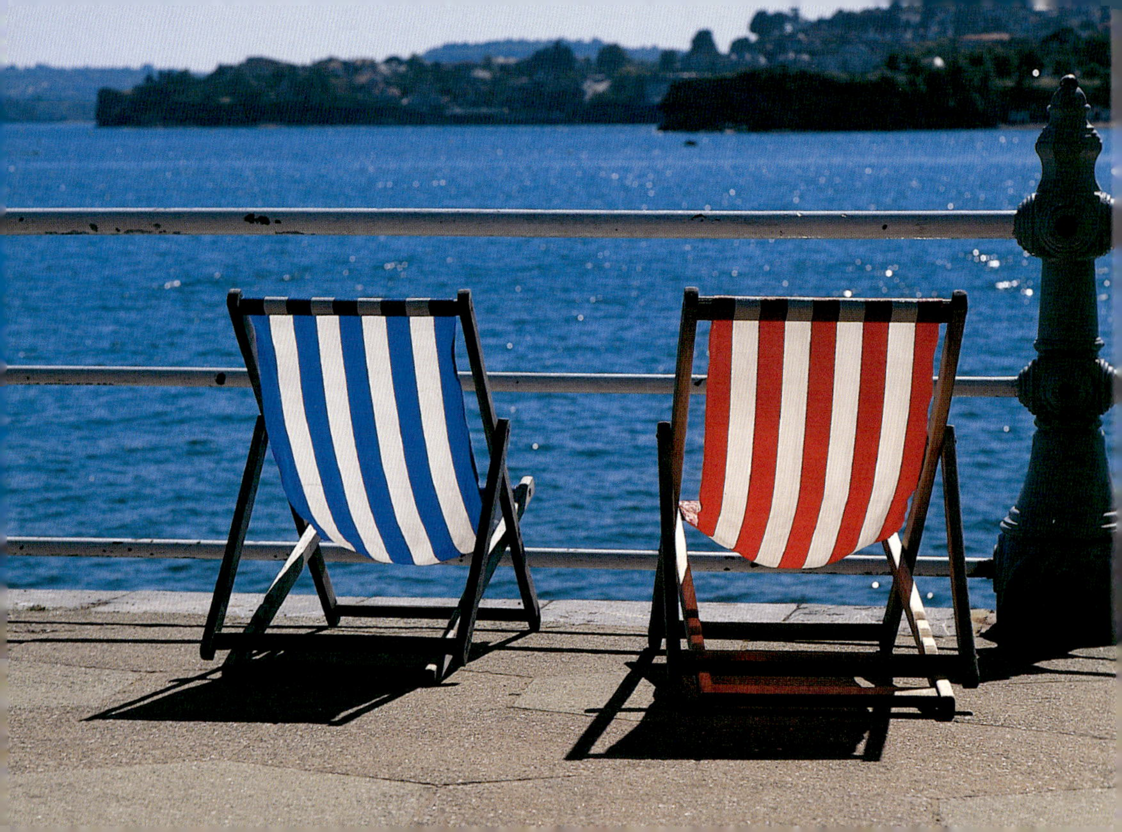